INCORRIGIBLE

A COMING-OF-AGE MEMOIR OF

LOSS, ADDICTION & INCARCERATION.

Wendy Adamson

ROTHCO PRESS • LOS ANGELES, CALIFORNIA

For my parents, Doug and Nancy.

Life can only be understood backwards;
but it must be lived forwards."
– Soren Kierkegaard

Table of Contents

CHILDHOOD

Family Time

The hospital looked more like a Mission than the mental institution it actually was. After an hour of driving up the coast with my family, past acres of farmland, we passed under an archway, onto the expansive grounds, then turned down a narrow road where Dad parked the station wagon.

"This is where Mommy's at?" I asked, leaning forward.

Bruce stirred at the sound of my voice. "Mommy's here?" He rubbed the sleep from his eyes.

"Yup," Dad said, twisting around in his seat. "And I want you kids to behave." His tanned face hard with parental expectation.

"Yes, Daddy," we all sing-songed.

No one wanted to upset him or else he might yell at us in front of strangers. In fact, earlier on the drive, Bruce and I had gotten into a silly argument and Dad extinguished it as quickly as he did his Camel cigarettes that he smoked back-to-back. Besides, we were all excited to be visiting Mom and had dressed in our Sunday best. My ten-year-old brother, Jay, sat up front. My eight-year-old sister, Diane, and my four-year-old brother Bruce, and six-year old me were all tucked in the back. Diane and I both had Dutch-boy bangs and pixie cuts that we had gotten at Dad's barber shop. Mom usually took care of our hair, but while she'd been away, Dad had taken the liberty of cutting it all off.

Uneasy, I shifted and stared out at the two-story building with black iron bars covering the windows. A pole with a California flag and a grizzly bear on all fours blew in the warm wind. The place was spooky. My heart raced inside my chest. I hadn't seen Mom for a month. And while I wanted to visit her, I was afraid she might be in one of her angry moods.

As soon as I stepped onto the asphalt, I felt the heat rising through the bottom of my shiny black shoes. My dress stuck to the back of my legs and I had to blink to adjust to the bright afternoon sun. When we got on the curb a gruffy man, with red-rimmed eyes shuffled by. I took my father's hand. "This place is creepy," I said.

"You say that about everything," Jay said.

"No, I don't. You do!"

"Knock it off you two," Dad said.

Dad led us up a path, our Sunday shoes clicked on the cement like deer. The massive door of the two-story building had green chipped paint and smudges of brown. Dad pushed a buzzer on an intercom that was about half the size of my lunchbox.

"Can I help you?"

Dad leaned toward the speaker. "We're here to visit Nancy Adamson."

A loud buzzer sounded and the lock released. Dad pushed with his shoulder and we stepped inside to a long corridor with buffed linoleum floors, lit up with overhead lights.

A pale nurse with a narrow face appeared. "Well, hello there, kiddos."

While I had been taught to respect adults in positions of authority, we were there for one reason only. "I want to see my Mommy."

"Good, because your Mommy wants to see you." She smiled revealing a gap between her front teeth.

A thin woman wearing a stained gown and slippers drifted by like a ghost. She gave me goose bumps, but when I looked up at my Dad, he seemed completely at ease. I figured it must be safe.

My family clustered together as we were led down the hall and into the dayroom. A television was blaring some show. Large chairs were arranged in rows with over a dozen people staring at the screen. A coffee table was covered with scattered puzzle pieces. I couldn't make out what the image was, but it looked like it resembled a mountain range.

"She's sitting right over there." The nurse pointed to my mother, who was dressed in a light pink smock, her hands resting daintily in her lap. She stared right through us.

A few months earlier Mommy had been making me a peanut butter and jelly sandwich in the kitchen at home when something weird happened. She was stunning, dressed in an A-line skirt and tailored blouse, with her long neck poking out of the collar. When she froze staring inside the fridge, I knew something was wrong. "He's trying to poison us," she said, grabbing the bottle of milk and pouring it down the sink.

"Mommy, what's wrong?" That's when she slammed the bottle down, sending shards of glass across the floor. When she stormed towards me, I wanted to run, but it was too late. She picked me up like a ragdoll and pushed me from behind, kneeing me in the back.

"Mommy, mommy, please don't..."

"You are a bad girl. A very bad girl. Don't you dare come out of your room." She shoved me into my bedroom and slammed the door. I curled up in a tight ball under my covers, wishing she were dead or at the very least, that she would just go away.

Now Mommy sat there in the dayroom, blinking several times until she finally recognized us.

"My babies!" When she stood up, she looked like herself again.

"Mommy!" I ran over and she folded me in her arms. I didn't want to let her go.

Dad gently tugged on my shoulder. "Let your brothers and sister say hello."

"I'm so happy to see you." My mother hugged all of us. "Come, come. Let's go sit outside."

Moments later we were sitting at one of the wooden picnic tables inside a walled-off courtyard. The table's surface was rough, splintered and carved up with letters. A few other families sat at nearby tables. I sat on one side of my mother, Diane sat on the other, with my brothers sitting across from us. I don't remember where Dad was, but I imagine him standing with his arms crossed over his chest like he always did. I also imagine his frustration with a wife whose instability left him to deal with four kids alone. I'm sure this was not the plan he had when they first had met.

I would be told later on that my grandfather, James, met my mother before she met my father, when she stood drenched in the rain at a Los Angeles train station. She was twenty-six at the time, and apparently, he felt sorry for her and asked her if she needed a ride. On the drive, my grandfather was so charmed by my mother, he wanted her to meet his thirty-three-year-old son, Doug. Arrangements were made and Dad and Mom went out on their first date. It was simple, really. Mom thought Dad was handsome with his dark hair and thin debonair moustache. It was love at first sight. Having been a bachelor until his thirties, Dad wanted to get married right away. The story goes that before my mother would say "yes" she insisted that all her children be raised Catholic. After he agreed, their elaborate wedding was held at St. Peter's church in downtown L.A. Soon after that, Dad started a real estate business that did so well, he was able to buy a ranch-style home in West Los Angeles.

"Do you like staying here, Mommy?" I asked.

"I'd much rather be home with you kids."

"When are you coming home?" Diane tugged on her arm.

Silence.

"Is this place for crazy people?" Jay asked.

"Jay!" Dad snapped, taking a step forward.

Something was off with Jay, but no one talked about that either. One time last year, he pounded me in the stomach with his fist three times for no apparent reason. Thus I learned at a very early age to keep a distance from him. We all did.

My eyes darted back and forth from Mom to Dad.

"It's a place for people who are struggling," Mom said. "And we all struggle at some point in our lives, Jay."

Although I knew something had changed between my parents, I was too young to know that Dad was threatening to get a divorce. Apparently, he was growing weary of his wife's constant breakdowns. By then my mother had been to the State Hospital many times, and the combination of shock treatments and medications didn't seem to be working at all.

After an hour, it was time to go.

"Come home with us, Mommy," I pleaded. "Please?"

"I can't right now." She glanced up at Dad. "But I'll be home soon."

Leaving my mother hurt my chest. I wanted her back home. She was the one who brushed my hair, gave me bubble baths, read to me, and took me to the park. I wanted to help her bake cookies in the kitchen and lick the bowl after. I wanted that Mommy to come home with me, not the one who thought the milk was poisoned.

In the angled light of late afternoon, my mother waved goodbye to us, her shoulders hunched over, a two-dimensional silhouette with a deep sadness behind her eyes. At the time, I had no idea what was wrong with her, but there was always some clamoring part of me that wanted to peek inside so I could have a better understanding of what was going on in her mind. And if I was able to understand, then maybe, just maybe, I could do something to fix her and my mother would come home to love and adore me like she once had.

*

Even though the doctors had said Mom was stable enough to come home, I always wondered how long before she'd go away again. At seven years old Mom's breakdowns were happening a lot.

After a month we had fallen back into our usual routine of going to mass every Sunday.

"Get dressed or we'll be late for church," mom said.

"Do I have to go?" I asked.

"You don't want to go to hell, do you?" She leaned over, her long elegant neck extended, her face inches from mine.

"No, Mommy." I lowered my head. Fear clamped down on my throat whenever internal damnation was brought into the conversation. I believed bad girls would burn in hell for the rest of eternity. I already felt bad sometimes, so I didn't want to take any more chances. I slipped on my Sunday dress, with the itchy white ruffles around the neck, and my tight black polished shoes. A few minutes later my siblings and I were piling into the car.

St. Timothy's church was only a mile from our house. It was where I got baptized and Diane received her Holy Communion. Our shoes clicked up the stairs to the massive carved doors. A statue of Mother Mary stared down at us on one side, and Joseph on the other. The doors opened into a hollow foyer with intricate patterned blue and maroon tiled floors. Each one of us dipped our fingertips into the vessel that held the holy water, and made the sign of the cross. Then we followed Mom down the narrow side aisle to a closed-off room with large viewing windows designed so loud children wouldn't disrupt the ceremony. As we sat in the front pew, the priest's drone of Latin boomed through the PA system. I had no idea what any of it meant, but it turns out, no one did.

I pulled on a loose thread on my dress as the priest's voice faded away. When I was bored, I could drum up worlds inside my mind. A favorite fantasy I had was a Pegasus horse I conjured up. The great white steed with his sweeping angelic wings would put me on his back and fly me over the clouds where the people below looked like ants. The Pegasus was my friend and could sense when I needed him. And as a kid, I needed him a lot.

When mass was finally over Mom herded us back to the car. On the drive she'd be talking to us about the sermon, which was the only part not in Latin.

"Did you hear what the Monsignor said? You children need to obey Mommy and Daddy or you'll end up going to purgatory."

I looked over at Diane whose pixie-cut head was bobbing up and down as Mom talked. Even to a seven-year-old the church seemed riddled with contradictions that only ended up confusing me more.

Once back home I would quickly put on play clothes so I could go outside. Most of the kids in the neighborhood didn't go to church. Instead they got to play during that hour that I was bored to tears. Older boys would be bouncing a basketball down a driveway. Diane's friends often played hopscotch in chalked squares on the sidewalk.

I would run across the street to find my best friend, Arpi who was fairly new to the neighborhood. She had almond-shaped eyes and cherub lips and moved here from Turkey because of political unrest. One time I asked her about what was going on in her country to make her family flee, but she pushed the air away with her hand saying no one talked about that anymore.

Arpi and I loved to play Cowboy and Indians. We had toy horses that had a smiling plastic heads attached to a top of a short broom stick which we'd tuck between our legs. "Giddy up. Giddy up," we'd yell, circling each other on the lawn.

Our day flew by like that as it often did and before I knew it Mom was yelling "Dinner!" from across the street. Diane, Bruce and I would have to stop playing and run home. Jay never went outside with the rest of us. He stayed in his room reading or studying chess.

Whenever I entered the house, I was on the look-out to see if Mom's eyes were scary, or was she talking to herself again. But more than all that I could feel her energy shift, and when that happened it seemed my mother was no longer there.

I joined my siblings at the dining table, swinging my feet underneath my seat. Just then the kitchen door scraped open and Dad came in dressed in his boxers and a t-shirt. The polio he had contracted as a kid had caused his one of his calves to shrink down to the size of a baseball bat. If he wasn't wearing his orthopedic brace, his whole body would lean to one side, in order to sweep the emaciated leg forward.

"Is the food ready yet?" he asked.

Gone were the days where Dad would give Mom a wink or a peck on the cheek.

"Yes, sir," Mom said, setting a plate in his place.

I was observing everything. I watched Mom. I watched Dad. I watched my brothers and sisters. I had to pay close attention at all times.

After dinner, on Sundays we all gathered around the T.V to watch Bonanza. We were the first ones in our neighborhood who had a colored television set. We used to invite our friends over, but not so much any-more. My belly was full as I laid on the floor next to Diane. Dad was in his recliner chair, and the boys were on the couch. All of the sudden Mom was standing be-hind us drying her hands on a dish towel. "Did you kids get out your uniforms out for school tomorrow?" she asked.

We all sighed.

"Damn it, Nancy. I'm trying to hear this show," Dad said.

"Stop yelling in front of the kids." Mom's voice matched his.

"Go get your clothes ready kids, and you can thank your mom for missing your favorite show." Droplets of spit sprayed from Dad's mouth.

We left but once in my room, I pressed my ear against the door in order to hear them. It didn't take long before Dad started saying things like "bitch' and 'crazy' and other words we weren't allowed to say. Mom's shrill voice pierced the air. And then there was a loud bang and another, and another. I had no idea what was going on, but I was afraid Dad might be hitting her. My body began to tremble, my hands shook. I looked over at my sister. "Why is Daddy so mean to Mommy?" I asked.

"I don't think they love each other anymore." Diane's voice cracked.

A few minutes later I heard the front door slam. Everything went silent, and I crawled into my bed.

*

In the middle of the night I woke up cradled in the arms of a fireman. His red-rimmed, shiny hat cast a shadow over his face. He rushed me down the hallway. The family photographs on the wall went by in a blur. My eyes burned and my throat was tight. The fireman burst out the front door where my entire family was huddled together. He set me down on the lawn next to my father. "Are you alright?" Dad asked, his brow creased. I was still half asleep. "Are you alright?" He asked again.

"What's going on, Daddy?"

"There was an accident, is all."

An accident could mean anything in our house from a broken glass, to something spilled on the carpet or one of the pets making a mess. But accidents usually meant something was wrong with Mom again. My toes gripped the moist grass as if I was trying to stay tethered to the earth. It's a habit I have to this day.

All of a sudden, the screen door flew open, and two paramedics pushed a gurney with Mom on it, arms strapped by her side. Her hazel eyes darted around like bees trapped inside a jar. Something primal stirred at the sight of my mother pinned down. I wanted to climb on top of the gurney and curl my body alongside hers, but fear kept me back. Fear always kept me back. Just then, Diane came over and draped a protective arm over my shoulder.

The wheels of the gurney clicked across the sidewalk to the ambulance that was parked in the middle of the street. The paramedics collapsed the gurney and lifted my mother into the vehicle, and then slammed the door.

The lights on top of the firetruck streaked red across our faces. Walkie talkies crackled. Street lamps illuminated the neighborhood. When the ambulance drove away, my eyes came back into focus like the eye of a camera coming into view. For the first time I noticed the neighbors watching us like we were on a stage. Mrs. Miller perched on her porch. Next door neighbor peeking out her window. We had been exposed. Now everyone on the entire block knew that Mom was sick. Crazy sick. I stood there shrinking and weightless, my mind a fractured kaleidoscope of jumbled thoughts. I felt like an insignificant speck of dust, that if a gentle wind came along it could blow me away.

There would be no explanation or conversations about what Mom had done or where she went that night. In fact, I wouldn't find out until years later that Dad had threatened her with divorce again before storming off to the local bar. Devastated, my mother closed all the windows and turned on the gas, trying to kill herself. I knew none of that at seven years old. But I did know that something was terribly wrong with all the adults in my house, and I wanted out.

*

Our babysitter, Vivian, was large with doughy flesh and aggressive moles on her nose and cheeks. Mom had been gone a month, and Vivian had been arriving every morning in her Hawaiian mu-mus to get us fed and off to school. Anytime she'd walk down the hallway one hand would brush the length of the wall for support. When she sat on the edge of my bed, her weight caused my body to roll toward her and collide with hers.

"Time to get up," she said.

I turned over on my back. "But I feel really sick."

She placed her fleshy hand on my forehead. "You don't have a fever."

"I still feel sick."

I didn't like going to school anymore. It was more important for me to stay home so I could keep an eye on things. If I wasn't there, anything could happen.

"If you're sick you won't be able to eat pancakes this morning."

I studied her face to see if she was for real. Adults had a way of tricking you if you weren't paying attention.

"Maybe the pancakes would make me feel better."

She patted me on the head like a Golden Retriever.

A few minutes later, I joined Bruce, Jay and Diane at the semi-circular breakfast nook. A huge stack of pancakes sat on a platter in the center of the table. Jay was wearing a corrective eyepatch because one eye had inadvertently gone inward. It always made it hard to look directly at him because you didn't know where he was looking.

Dad came in, already dressed for work in his baggy pants, white shirt and tweed blazer.

"Coffee, Mr. A?" Vivian asked.

"Yes please," he said, scooting into the booth.

Vivian set down a cup of steamy hot coffee in front of dad. I sliced butter and carefully inserted it between each layer of pancakes. Then I drenched them all with a heap of maple syrup. At some point during breakfast I asked, "When is Mommy coming home?"

There was silence. Everyone looked over at Dad.

"Soon. She'll be back soon."

That was the only answer he gave. It didn't stop me from prying more.

"But when?"

"Look, you kids need to get ready for school," he said, with a wave of his hand.

"But Daddy..."

"Enough!" he snapped.

And that was it. End of discussion.

*

Being the child of a sick mother meant either longing for her to love me, or wishing she were dead. Every time she hit me or washed my mouth out with soap I wanted her to die or at the very least, go away. And then came the day when my father took me to my favorite drive-in diner to give me the news.

"Can you keep a secret?" he began. "I don't want you telling Bruce because he's too young to know. You hear me?"

I was seven years old and well trained in keeping secrets.

"I promise, Daddy I won't tell."

"Your mommy had a heart attack and won't be coming home again."

I sucked in a deep breath. That didn't seem possible. Mommy went away a lot, but she always came back. Why was it different this time? Death had instantly moved into the realm of reality, and I had so many questions that I couldn't form inside my mind. Questions like: Where did my mother go? Where was her body at? Why wasn't there a funeral like the ones I had seen on T.V.? But the most important question of them all was, how do I live in the world without my mother? How will I do my life?

In that moment, I wanted my Dad to hold me. I wanted him to tell me everything would be okay. But all I remember him saying was,"Remember not to tell Bruce."

After we drove back, Dad let me off in front of the house saying he had to get back to work. His Beverly Hills real estate business was thriving at the time and kept him away from home a lot. As I stood there and watched him drive off, it felt like he had pulled the pin out of a grenade and handed it to me. When I saw my friend Tommy playing across the street, I ran over and held him by both arms saying, "My mommy is dead." His pale blue eyes looked confused, so I said it again. "My mommy is dead." He squirmed away and ran inside. Then I told Susie. "My mommy is dead." I told everyone else I could find on the block that day. "My mommy is dead." What I didn't know then, was that I was looking for clues in their faces, in their reactions, that would indicate how a girl should feel when her mother wasn't coming home.

At the same time, I had another disturbing secret. I believed if I hadn't made all those stupid requests to God maybe my mother would still be there with me.

I was the reason my mother was dead, and that was a secret I would never tell.

The Move

A year later Vivian placed a steaming pot roast and biscuits on the table, before shuffling back into the kitchen. Dad sat at the head of the table with all us his children surrounding him.

"I got good news, kids," he said. "We're going to be moving."

I let out a gasp. One of my fantasies was that some-day my mother would walk in the front door with a big smile on her face. She would wrap me in her arms and tell me not to cry, that her dying had just been a huge misunderstanding. If we moved, I was worried that she would never be able to find us again.

"What do you mean?" Diane asked.

"I bought us a new home in Santa Monica."

"But all our friends live here," I said.

"You can make new friends." He picked up his fork and stuck it into the roast.

Macolm Avenue was a children's paradise for an eight-year-old, made only more idyllic by how familiar it was. I knew all the kids on the block, and their parents. I knew the exact time when the Millers peach tree was giving fruit. I knew nasty Eddie was always trying to get the girls in his garage so he could kiss them on the lips. I knew which dogs were friendly and which ones to stay clear of. I knew all the clerks that worked at the small convenience store down the block and they knew me. Our neighborhood was even safe to play Red Rover or dodge ball well into the soft light of dusk.

"The new house has a swimming pool," Dad said.

"I don't care. I want to stay here."

I tended to haggle, and usually wouldn't let up until Dad got so frustrated that he would cave in. This time was different. I begged and begged for us to stay there, but the deal had already been sealed. Quite literally, escrow had closed. We were leaving, like it or not.

Right before summer break, we boxed, labeled and stacked everything on top of each other, cardboard mountains in the living room. What was left of Mom's clothing was given to the Goodwill, along with our Kool-Aid stained couch, and an old television set.

The moving company came and loaded up a truck the day before. When I saw my bedroom looking like an empty box, I felt just as hollow. Diane and I slept in sleeping bags on the floor and commiserated over our disdain for Dad.

The next day Dad's station wagon was waiting by the curb, with an old wooden trailer hitched to the back. Friends had gathered on the sidewalk to say goodbye. Diane wiped away tears with the back of her hand. Bruce looked completely crushed, while I wanted to grab the nearest street post and hold on for dear life.

I shuffled back and forth, and when it came time to hug Arpi, my narrow shoulders shook with sobs.

Dad was inhaling a cigarette. I must have been taking too long, so he put a hand on my shoulder. "You'll get to see each other again. You can take the bus over here."

I had never taken a bus alone in my life—the thought was terrifying, my little body being surrounded by much taller strangers.

I looked at Arpi. "Dad says the number 8 blue bus can bring me all the way over here," I said. Our new house was only six miles from Malcolm Avenue, but as a small kid it might as well have been an entire continent.

"Call me." Hope was written all over Arpi's face.

"I will. I will."

As we piled in the car, we all waved, except Jay, who'd been friendless his entire life. I didn't know then that I would never see my friends again. As we drove away one of the windows was cracked, causing a high pitch whistle that got louder as we picked up speed. I watched the unfamiliar landscape. At one point, Dad's eyes accidentally met mine in the rear-view mirror. I looked away, determined to punish him for making us leave our beloved home. The only place I had ever known. The place that connected me to all the memories I had of my mother. The place where she could find me if she were still alive.

Without traffic, it took us about eleven minutes to get there.

Dad turned the car down 18th Street where it was lined with palm trees leaning west and every house seemed to have an expensive car parked in its driveway.

"Look at all these beautiful homes." Dad waved his hand.

"I don't see any kids." My eyes scanned back and forth.

"They're probably all inside right now."

Dad turned into a driveway. "Here we go kiddos," he said.

We all stared at the yellow house with a sloping, manicured lawn. Brown shutters framed the windows, a red brick porch with a painted white iron bench sat in the corner. A house that Dad could only afford because his Real Estate business was thriving, with all his movie start clients.

"Let's go check it out," Dad said.

We all begrudgingly followed dad up the path. After he opened the door with his shiny new key, we entered into a living room.

"Look at all the new furniture I bought." A sleek blue couch, a brand-new leather recliner and a television sat with a massive brick fireplace and mantel to the side. Obviously, he had been preparing for the move. Like the aggressive real estate agent that he was, Dad showed us the rest of the house. It was indeed impressive. It had three bedrooms on one side, a maid's quarters, laundry room, and a kitchen on the other side. A massive lanai sat in the back with a sliding glass door that let you out to a swimming pool that had a diving board.

I would discover that in this new neighborhood, kids didn't play on the streets. They were too busy going to ballet, music lessons, or other arranged extra-curricular activities. As a result, the entire block remained a ghost town, and I, the designated ghost.

The Help

Three years had passed since my mother's death, and I was depressed, even though I didn't know what it was back then. At ten years old I found it hard to make new friends, so I took to watching reruns of I Love Lucy in my room. One evening I had gone to the kitchen to get a handful of cookies and milk. Dad, as usual, was sitting in his recliner in the living room with a glass of vodka clutched in his hand. I was just about to slip down the hall when he stopped me.

"Wendy, come have a seat for a minute, will ya?"

His tone had a somber ring to it. I could always tell when he was about to deliver bad news, and unfortunately in my short life, there had been a lot of it. Trepidation swirled through my body, as I sat on the edge of our new couch. For the first time I noticed how his face looked like he had aged ten years since mom's death.

"I'm going to have to let Vivian go," he said.

I felt like I was sucker-punched. (It always felt like Dad was trying to remove any links to my mother and the past.) I reflected on all the years Vivian had been with us. She was the one who took care of me whenever mom would go away. The one who'd cook us pancakes and get us all ready for school in the mornings, tucking hands through sleeves, smoothing bangs. She wasn't perfect by any means, but I knew one thing, she loved us all.

"But why?"

"Your cousin Nicky from England is moving to the States, so I said she could come work for us."

"You never said anything about a cousin from England before."

"It never came up."

"But, but where will Vivian go?"

"She'll go live with her daughter."

"But, but... that's not fair."

"I don't have a choice. Nicky is family."

"When is she leaving?"

"The end of the month."

I knew his decision had already been made. There was no point in stating my objections. Instead, I stormed off to my room and climbed onto the bed to sulk. I held on to my stuffed teddy bear and pulled on his button eye, having the urge to destroy something. I tugged so hard that it popped off, leaving my favorite animal with one eye. I was instantly filled with regret. "I'm sorry, Teddy," I whispered.

Later that night, Dad opened the door and peeked inside. He flashed me a look like he was going to say something. His face hovered there, backlit by the hall lamp, and then he walked away.

The next few weeks with Vivian were hard. Whenever Dad wasn't around, she'd get all weepy. One day she was dabbing a tissue under her eyes when she told me how much she was going to miss me. I wanted to say something to relieve her pain.

"But you can come visit us."

"If my daughter has the time to give me a ride." She sniffled. "Everyone is so busy these days."

When the day finally arrived, Vivian's daughter showed up in her clunky black Chevy, her hair pulled back in a ponytail. I couldn't breathe as my siblings and I stood on the sidewalk with Dad. The two women put all of Vivian's belongings into the trunk. Vivian was dressed in one of her usual Hawaiian muu muus. She sobbed, making horrible shrieking sounds. I was in shorts and a t-shirt, nervously shifting back and forth. Diane was crying next to me. Why hadn't we appreciated Vivian all the years she had been with us? We complained to Dad about her being overweight and her constant nose picking. I would have taken it all back if she could have just stayed. I didn't yet understand that it's only in someone's absence that we feel the extent of our love.

The sun beat down on my neck as the neighbor's station wagon cruised by with a family staring at us from their open windows. The mom sitting shotgun with her long brown hair spinning in the wind, the father driving. A daughter about my age was in the back seat with a smile on her face. That's what a normal family should look like.

Vivian folded me into her arms. "I'm going to miss you so much," she said.

"Me too." I swallowed hard.

I usually hated Vivian's hugs because I could feel all the layers of flesh under her muu muu, but this time I leaned into her soft body. This time I didn't want to let her go. When it was Diane's turn to say goodbye, Vivian's shoulders were trembling. Bruce was crying, but Jay stood by not shedding a single tear.

Finally, Vivian lowered herself into the passenger's seat while her daughter climbed in behind the wheel. As she drove off, we were clustered together, waving good-bye. We waved until the taillights were out of view. That was the last time I saw Vivian. Little did I know that the goodbyes would begin to take their toll, as the people I loved always seemed to go away.

*

We were all gathered in the living room when Nicky arrived, dragging a shipping trunk like the one my mother used to have. She was in her early thirties, with thick red-orange hair that cascaded over her shoulders and bright, unblemished white skin.

"Well, hello." She leaned over as we sat on the couch.

With my arms crossed, I barely met her gaze. I had made up my mind I wasn't going to like her no matter what.

On the other hand, Dad was thrilled. "We're so glad you're here," he beamed.

"Well, I had to come meet my American cousins," she said, with a thick British accent.

There was an awkward silence as she smiled at all of us.

"How about we get you settled into your room?" Dad was already pulling the trunk towards the maid's quarters on the other side of the house. Diane and I took it as an opportunity to get away from Bruce and Jay and head to our bedroom. I plopped down on the edge of my bed and looked up at my older sister.

"What do you think of her?"

"She seems alright." Diane shrugged.

As the days passed, I tried my best not to like Nicky, but after a month my resolve was starting to crack. Who wouldn't be impressed? Nicky was sophisticated, worldly and had the same sexy accent that the Beatles had. Soon, I found myself asking her questions. Like: had she ever been to Liverpool? Had she ever heard the Beatles live and had she ever watched those Beatle songs come out of the cute mouths of John and Paul?

It was summer and we developed a daily routine of swimming or laying out by the pool with Nicky, who would make us peanut butter and jelly sandwiches for lunch. Nicky was much younger than Vivian and therefore much more active. She loved swimming laps, her long arms curving in and out of the water, while her feet propelled her across the pool.

After a couple months it became clear that Nicky had another reason to come to the United States. She was determined to find herself a rich, American husband. A steady stream of men showed up at our front door every night to take her out. I could tell it irritated my father. He made sarcastic comments after she would leave. But I was intrigued by Nicky's ability to attract so many eligible bachelors. How does she do it? Was it the accent? The red hair?

One day, Nicky took Diane and I to the beach. Jay and Bruce stayed behind because they weren't interested in getting a tan or hanging out with lame girls.

Once we arrived at State Beach, Nicky would have us lay our towels out in her favorite spot by the volleyball courts. That way she could prop herself up on her elbows and watch the boys curl their lean, tanned bodies into C's as they slammed the ball over the net, abs contracting, arms outstretched.

I remember Nicky's slinky navy-blue bikini bordered with white eyelet trim. She didn't seem to care that her pale skin never tanned, while Diane and I would turn a golden brown. Just the same, lying next to her in my one piece she made me want to shrivel up. I don't know where it came from but ever since I can remember I had a disdain for my thick thighs and pudgy belly that made me want to hide. Diane never had a problem with weight like I did, but then again, she never wolfed down Oreos before she went to bed. But Nicky was different than both of us. She was not only in her body, she flaunted it.

I studied Nicky as if she held all the secrets I would need to navigate the male species later on. When a cute boy with colorful Hawaiian trunks walked by and Nicky held his gaze, I took a mental note.

With the sun beating down, Diane and I were getting hot, so we went down to the edge of the water to cool off. Diane wasn't afraid to go out past the waves but I'd only go in up to my waist.

"Come on out!" Diane yelled, beyond the breakers.

I'm okay right here."

When I turned around Nicky was talking to the boy in the colorful trunks. Even then, I somehow knew she was using her body as a means to lure in men. I figured she used her body to meet all her dates.

Eventually, Diane came out of the water and we headed back. I shook out the sand from my towels and wrapped it around me. Nicky was leaning up on her elbows watching the boys play the game.

"I'm tired," I said. "Can we go home now?"

"Yeah, Nicky can we go?"

Reluctantly, Nicky started packing everything up into an oversized straw bag.

"We're going to walk home today," she said.

"What?" I couldn't believe my ears.

"But it's too far," Diane said.

"Walking is good exercise for you girls," Nicky insisted.

It didn't make any sense to walk when we could easily catch the bus home. We were even more shocked when Nicky decided to wear her skimpy bikini on the busy San Vicente Boulevard. While two-piece bathing suits were openly worn on the beach in the sixties, no one dared to make such a public display of that much flesh on a public street. Diane, being a good Catholic girl, shook her head in disgust as we trailed behind her sashaying form. We hadn't even gone two blocks when I started complaining.

"Nicky, can't we just catch the bus?"

"This is a nice little walk. You'll be fine."

Just then a shiny black Jaguar pulled over to the curb. The passenger window went down and a man in his forties yelled out, "Can I give you ladies a lift?"

A smile stretched out across Nicky's face when she said, in her sexiest British accent. "That would be lovely."

"But we're not supposed to take rides..." Diane said.

"You were just complaining about being tired so here we are." Nicky waved her hand toward the car, just as the stranger threw open the passenger door. Our young mouths hung open as Nicky approached him with her hips sashaying in an exaggerated fashion.

We had been warned by Dad to never, ever, no matter what to get into a car with a stranger. Ever. But here was our British cousin who seemed insistent on ushering us towards danger for an untimely death.

"Come on girls," Nicky said. "Let's not keep the gentleman waiting."

Mortified, we walked over as the man tilted the front seat forward and we had no choice but to get in. As I glanced up at the creepy driver my breath felt stuck inside my throat.

"Well hell-ooo girls," he said, in a sing-songy voice.

Even though he didn't look like a pervert per se, I was suspicious. Dad had warned us that kidnappers can often look like the guy next door. That they used their ordinary appearances along with candy, puppies, or other tantalizing gifts to lure innocent children to get into their unmarked white vans. It hadn't even taken one piece of milk chocolate to get us all into his car.

With Diane and I trapped in the back, Nicky lowered her bikini-clad bum onto the smooth leather of the front seat. Diane kept throwing elbows into my ribs.

"Thanks for the ride." Nicky said, batting her lashes. "The girls were just saying how tired they are."

"Glad I could help," he said. "Where you headed?"

"Just up to 18th Street."

"Well, let's get you home then." The car hummed as he stepped on the gas.

Diane socked me on the thigh with her balled up fist. I rolled my eyes up to the heavens and shrugged. All the grown-ups were crazy and there was nothing anyone could do to change that fact.

"Are these your girls?" He glanced back at us.

"Oh no." Nicky giggled. "I'm their cousin and take care of them during the day while their father's at work."

"That's very nice of you," he said.

I didn't know anything about sex, but I could almost smell the hormones swirling throughout the car.

"Can I call you sometime then?" he asked.

"Oh. I would love that," Nicky tilted her head, one shoulder dipping down.

He reached into the middle console and pulled out a pen and piece of paper and handed it to Nicky. She scribbled her number and handed it back to him just as we were pulling up in front of our house.

"I look forward to hearing from you," Nicky said, opening the passenger door.

"I look forward to seeing you again, Nicky." His eyes were filled with a longing I didn't quite understand.

"Bye girls," he said, as we leaped from the car, grateful for our limbs intact.

*

Diane was furious and later when Dad got home from work she told him what Nicky had done. Immediately, Dad stormed into the kitchen to confront Nicky as Diane and I hid in the next room to eavesdrop.

"You got in a strange man's car with my girls?" he yelled.

"The girls were complaining they were tired so I thought..."

He cut her off, "What's wrong with the goddamn bus?"

"I thought some exercise would do them good."

"How about exercising some self-restraint around men?"

As his voice echoed throughout the house, Diane held onto my arm. We grew up with our parents fighting all the time, and dad got mean when he was mad. I braced myself for the worst.

"How dare you," Nicky said.

"Get the hell out of my house."

"The kids should know that I'm not really their cousin, and that you made it up to get Vivian out of your house."

My mouth fell open as I looked at Diane. We both shook our heads in disbelief. Nicky wasn't our cousin? Dad had lied? Diane's eyes looked like they were going to come clear out of the sockets. There were things in the house that didn't make sense, fraying threads.

"Get the hell out of here!" Dad's voice echoed off the walls.

"My pleasure. I'm sick of washing your filthy underwear anyway," Nicky snapped.

Just then my brothers came out to investigate as Diane and I were heading back to our room. "Dad's a liar," I said, as I passed them.

"What? What are you talking about?" Bruce said.

"Nicky's not our cousin. Dad made it up."

Diane and I stormed down the hall to our room, slamming the door.

Fury gripped my body. I wanted to yank at the loosening threads, to see how much more of our family history would come undone.

I often wondered how Dad found Nicky in the first place. Did he run an ad in the Times or hire a service to find someone suitable to raise kids? All I know, is later my Dad would defend his actions because he said he didn't want to hurt Vivian's feelings. He also thought it would be easier for all of us to accept Nicky if she were a family member. But I can't help but think that he probably wanted to save face, so he created a scenario where his hands were tied. After all, doesn't family always come first?

Within an hour one of Nicky's boyfriends came to pick her up. When Nicky came to say goodbye, dad stood with his arms crossed in front of her chest.

"Goodbye girls," her eyes glistened with tears. "I'm going to miss you."

I had really started to like Nicky. But just like everyone else, she too, was full of shit. I never saw our made-up cousin again.

*

No matter how much Dad checked references, or interviewed potential housekeepers, he always seemed to hire the craziest of the lot. I can't count how many babysitters, nannies or housekeepers we had growing up, but clearly, someone else should have been doing the hiring.

After Nicky left, Pearl, a southern Black woman, with coffee bean skin and a big smile moved in. There was something familiar about Pearl. She was warm and really tried to connect with us kids during the day, but the nights were a different story altogether.

After everyone was tucked into their beds, Diane and I would hear a soft knock on our door and Pearl would peer inside. "Will one of you girls come sleep in my room?" she'd whisper.

"No, Pearl," Diane said.

"There's spirits in there."

Chills ran through my body. I pulled the covers up to my chin. The maid's bedroom was behind the kitchen on the other side of our U-shaped house. Nothing fancy, but comfortable enough, with a bed, a television, a dresser and its own bathroom. So far, none of the other housekeepers reported spirits back there, but maybe Pearl could see things like I had when I was a kid. At five years old I was convinced something resided in the wicker laundry basket under my bed. Every night after my mother or father tucked me in, I would sense a presence in the room. When I got ready to yell for someone to help me, its long skinny arms and legs would shoot up from underneath both sides of the bed and pin me down. Long, gray fingers would cover my mouth so I couldn't scream. Although I couldn't prove it, I knew there were monsters that preyed on children when parents weren't paying attention. But, like most kids, I was told I had an active imagination, and when they moved me in to my sister's room, I stopped having the night terrors.

"We're trying to sleep, Pearl," Diane said.

Lowering her scarved head, Pearl gently closed the door.

"Is she seeing ghosts back there?" I asked.

"No," Diane said, turning to face the wall. "Now, go back to sleep."

"But what if there are ghosts in our house?"

"There's no such thing as ghosts."

We told Dad about Pearl's visits to our room and after several months he let her go, then soon after that he hired Anne. Anne was in her forties, and for some reason that I can't pinpoint she gave me the feeling that she didn't like kids. But she was good at organization and performing the household duties. None of us would ever learn how to cook or clean or do anything most children do while growing up. Occasionally, I was told to make my bed, but that was about it.

It didn't take long before Anne started having a cocktail with Dad in the living room. When they sat together, I could tell she was more interested in his stories than she was with any of us. Although we didn't know it, Anne was developing a crush on her boss. I suppose to a single working woman, Dad would have been considered a catch. He had a thriving real estate business and could be quite the charmer when he wanted to be. But other than Doris, a part-time, elusive girlfriend who came on the scene a couple years after Mom died, Dad didn't seem interested in getting married again, or at least that's what he said.

Anne was with us nearly a year when one day I got home from school and she was nowhere to be found. That was strange because she always had snacks ready for us on the table in the afternoon. But on this particular day, there was just an empty, eerie silence in the house. I thought maybe she had gone to the market, so I started pulling out an English muffin and peanut butter to make my own snack. That's when I noticed the toaster was not on the counter where it usually was. I started looking in the cabinets to see if Anne had put it away. Then I noticed the waffle maker was gone, and so was the radio that Dad had bought for the kitchen. I turned and went through the adjacent laundry room to her bedroom in the back. My heart started to race when I saw the television was gone and so were all her clothes that had been in the closet. I rushed back to the dining room to call Dad. My hands were shaking when I picked up the phone and dialed his work. I told his secretary it was urgent and I needed to talk to him, now. When he finally came to the phone, I said, "I think Anne robbed us."

"What? What do you mean?"

"All her stuff is gone from her room and so is the television set."

"I'll be right there."

When Dad got home, he quickly assessed the situation before calling the police. He made an official report, but we never got any of our things back. It wouldn't be until I was in my 20s that I'd run into Anne again. I was detoxing from heroin in a small local hospital and she was in the next bed for a gall bladder surgery. I didn't recognize her at first, but then again, I was sick. When the nurse came in to give me some meds, she said my last name to make sure I was the right patient. After the nurse left, my roommate said, "I used to know an Adamson, his name was Doug."

I lifted my head and squinted as if seeing her for the first time. She looked vaguely familiar, but I couldn't quite place her.

"That's my dad."

"Oh goodness. My name is Anne. I worked for your family a long time ago."

Instantly, my thoughts went back to the day I came home when everything was gone. Part of me wanted to interrogate her right there in her hospital beds as to why she pulled the heist. Was she falling for my Dad? Was she jealous of Doris? But my whole body ached from the heroin leaving my cells, and besides, I now stole to support my habit. So, who was I to judge?

"I remember who you are." I laid my head back on the pillow.

After Anne robbed us, there were a few months when we were on our own. Dad was struggling, trying to run a thriving business while also trying to run the house. After countless interviews, when I was 11 years old Dad hired Irene, an Irish woman who had flaming red hair with a sweeping lower chin that looked like a ski-jump.

I will never forget Irene's first day when she cooked Irish stew with buttermilk biscuits. It was hard to understand what she was saying with her thick Irish brogue, and I found myself trying to read her lips.

"You like the stew, sweetie?" she asked.

"Yeah, it's okay," Looking down, I was determined not to get close to any more housekeepers because they all turned out to be nuts.

"You know Irene worked for Zsa Zsa Gabor," Dad said.

Zsa Zsa was a well-known Hungarian actress at the time.

"You worked for Zsa Zsa?" Bruce asked.

"I did, until she fired me because I used too much garlic in the food," Irene laughed.

In spite of trying to keep my distance, over the next few years, Irene would grow on me. It was her humor and wit that made me fall in love with the Irish. And while Irene liked to drink, she would never see spirits in her room, take us in cars with strangers, or steal our kitchen appliances, but the more she turned into Dad's drinking buddy, the more she'd reveal things we weren't supposed to know.

*

Sundays in Beverly Hills at Uncle Hal and Aunt Gretchen's house were an exercise in restraint for the entire family. There were specific instructions not to bicker or tease each other. No fighting. Instead it was an opportunity for us to implement those ever-elusive common courtesies, practice table manners, and for dad to present the best version of himself that he possibly could. A few years later, these dinners would also be the setting for Uncle Hal to write a hefty check because dad would be on the brink of bankruptcy, but in 1964, they were both doing great.

Dad's brother, Harold, was a successful lyricist with a career that spanned 40 years. In the early 30's he wrote songs for Broadway shows. In 1933, he signed a contract with MGM and moved to Hollywood. Harold had been nominated for five Academy Awards for songs such as "An Affair to Remember," "Around the World in 80 Days," and "A Lovely Way to Spend an Evening," to name a few.

Gretchen used to be a stage actress on Broadway. She looked the part: porcelain skin, emerald green eyes, and lashes that curled up to her arched eyebrows. Gretchen was fun and would take Diane and me to see movies like Mary Poppins and 101 Dalmatians, and even took Bruce fishing to a nearby lake at times. Despite her starlet's beauty, Gretchen was the closest thing to a stable woman I had ever known. She seemed genuinely interested in how I was doing. She asked questions like, "Do you miss your mom?" and said things like, "If you ever want to talk, I'm here for you." I might have told her that I felt sad, only we had been programmed by

Dad not to talk about my mother, and I'm sure that I would not have had the words.

Dad would pull into the driveway and park his Buick in front of the pool house. Before we got out of the car, he'd warn us: "No fighting, kids. You hear me?"

"Yes Dad," we'd all answer in unison.

The back yard was a sanctum of privilege with a massive wall of ivy that blocked any nosy neighbors from gazing in. My siblings and I followed Dad past the kidney-shaped pool, framed by a luscious lawn where we played competitive games of croquet. Daffodils lined the walkway and when a breeze hit them just right, they bowed like a line of curtsying women. We'd file up the two steps entering into Hal's study where we were all greeted with pecks on the cheeks.

"Hi, Uncle Hal, hi, Aunt Gretchen."

The den was where we spent the first part of the evening, unless of course Hal had a new song to debut. Then we'd parade into the expansive white living room where Hal would use the Steinway piano to perform. Sadly, like the two other Adamson brothers, Hal had contracted polio as a kid, leaving one hand partially paralyzed, while Dad had it in his leg. In order for Uncle Hal to play, he'd guide his limp right hand with his left, a technique he'd mastered by his late fifties.

Just the week before this Hal had played us a song he had written for an upcoming movie starring Don Knotts. He was really excited because it was the only movie he had done for kids.

"Don Knotts will sing this song in the movie." Hal lifted his right hand and his index finger hit the first note as he sang the lyrics he'd written:

I wish
I wish
I wish I were a fish
'Cause fishes have a better life than people...

While Hal was singing, my gaze drifted over the fireplace to the painting of Minnie, my paternal grandmother, captured in a white lace blouse with her hands folded elegantly in her lap. I had only met her a few times before she died, but apparently her sons missed her very much because they talked about her all the time. On the other wall was a painting of a red brick Tudor house located in Larchmont Shores, New York where Dad spent some of his childhood before moving to Brooklyn. Or maybe it was the other way around?

But on this particular visit with Hal not having any new songs we were all back sitting in the den. As usual, it started with cocktails for the grownups and sodas for the kids.

"What would you like to drink, darling?" Gretchen asked.

"I'll have a Coke with cherries please," I said.

After each of us had a glass in our hands, we'd all sit around for pleasantries. Gretchen was trying to quit smoking, so she always held a plastic cigarette, which gave her something to do with her hands. The sophisticated way she held it out between her slender fingers made it seem like a prop.

"How ya kids doing in school?" Harold asked.

"I'm getting straight A's." Jay was a bragger when it came to academics.

During one of these visits, I had revealed to Gretchen that I wanted to be an actress. At the time I had become enamored by Barbara Eden of I Dream of Jeannie and Shirley McLean in The Apartment. Like girls all across the world, native Angelenos were not immune to the seductive glamor of Hollywood. The escapism, for a young girl like myself working hard to compartmentalize grief, was appealing. When I told Gretchen, her face brightened with excitement. She said she'd love to give me acting lessons.

So, every week after drinks, while my brothers and sister played croquet on the lawn, Gretchen took me out to the pool house for lessons. It was a small one bedroom with framed posters from blockbuster movies all over the walls. Vintage vases held fresh bouquets of flowers. A wooden Victrola AM radio sat on an end table. A small bar held glasses with gold leaf trim and a matching ice bucket. I sat next to Gretchen on a sage green, overstuffed love seat.

"Now, darling, every actress absolutely needs to know how to cry," she said, placing a gentle hand on my knee. "Try thinking of something sad."

There was an irony in this request, given she knew my family history. But even when I scrunched my forehead, pouted my lips, the tears wouldn't come.

"I can't do it," I said, frustrated.

"It's okay, dear. Watch me." Gretchen's face contorted as she drifted somewhere else. In less than a minute her eyes glazed over with tears.

I was impressed.

"All I have to do is think about my mother who died when I was a little girl."

She looked at me pointedly as she said this, adult eyes searching my little girl face. I didn't get what she was doing. I didn't understand the bridge she was trying to build between us.

"Now. Try thinking of something that makes you sad," she said.

My throat closed up. I squished my brow together trying to force the tears, but still- nothing came.

Somewhere in my short life, I'd grown determined to bury the scared, little girl I had become. Addicted to fantasy, I sometimes dreamed of being a beautiful model on a shiny cover of a fashion magazine. Other times, I wanted to sing like Judy Garland when she belted out Somewhere Over the Rainbow. If fans adored me for my talents, then maybe I wouldn't feel like I needed to apologize for taking up so much space in the world.

"I can't do this," I said, lowering my head.

"It's okay darling. We can try a different emotion. How about showing me what it looks like when you're mad?"

"Mad." I nodded.

I scrunched up my forehead again. I tightened my little hands into balled fists, digging my fingernails into my palms. A part of me aimed to draw blood. I narrowed my eyes. My lips became nothing more than a slit. Anger was an emotion I could easily access, and over time I would gain even more expertise.

"Yes! Yes! Yes!" Gretchen said, holding a fearful hand to her chest. "I'm scared. You look really, really mad."

Proud of myself, I smiled.

Looking back, Gretchen's impact on my life was subtle, yet profound. I think ultimately that our bond was far deeper than any mutual interest in acting, but more about the physical and emotional fracture a girl feels when losing a mother at an early age. While Gretchen could access her grief through acting, she was probably trying to teach me how to do the same. But growing up in an atmosphere of secrecy with Dad not wanting anyone to know about his wife's mental illness, I had begun to shut down. And while I never confided in Gretchen, perhaps if I had, I might have connected with her deeper and not have felt so all alone.

Later that same evening while driving home on Sunset Boulevard, I ignored the chatter of my brothers and sisters, and gazed out the window. Along the highway hung dreams of signing my own contract with MGM or, at the very least, becoming someone else.

Hormones

I was thirteen and sitting in a classroom at St. Monica's when I felt the warm gush between my thighs. I had just turned thirteen and thought I might have peed on myself. I raised my hand to be excused. A quick nod from the nun and I was rushing down the aisle out the back door. The corridor was empty as I made my way to the girls' bathroom. Once inside the stall, I lifted my thick wool skirt and pulled my yellow-day-of the week panties down although it might have been the wrong day. I thought I might die. The crotch was saturated with bright red blood.

In a normal household, girls would learn about periods from their mothers. But since I didn't have a mother or a normal household, I never got the memo. What I did learn was from the school yard mostly. I remember hearing a girl talking about how she got her period, but I never asked any questions because I didn't want to appear stupid.

As I sat there on the cold toilet seat, I wished Diane would come in and give me some sisterly advice. But the last time we bumped into each other in that same bathroom she yelled at me to leave her alone when I tried to talk to her. Even her friend Patty told her to stop being so mean to me. At 16 she was embarrassed and didn't want to have anything to do with me because

I was turning into a rebellious Catholic girl and she was the compliant one.

My only option was to roll up a wad of toilet paper around my hand, and stuff it in the crotch of my panties. I checked the blue and gray plaid skirt. It hadn't seeped through, so I went back to class. I couldn't concentrate on the rest of the lessons because I kept thinking I might be bleeding out.

Later I found my best friend Laura standing near the volleyball courts.

"I'm bleeding. Down there," I said, full of shame.

She shrugged.

"I don't know what to do."

"You can either wear a sanitary napkin or use a tampon."

"What do you use?"

"I use tampons," she said. "I don't like the feeling of having a saddle between my legs."

"Where do I get one of these... tampons?"

"Come over after school. I'll give you some."

At 3:00 Laura and I walked to her house. As soon as I walked in, I smelled the Pine Sol.

"Is that you, Laura?" her mom, yelled from the other room.

"Yeah, mom, I got Wendy with me. I'm going to show her how to use a tampon."

"Laura!"

She waved a dismissive hand just as her mother appeared, hair coiffed, with a smile on her face. "Oh Laura, that's so sweet of you. You're such a good friend," she said, hands over her heart.

"Thanks Mom. We're going upstairs."

Humiliated, I followed Laura up the winding staircase to the bathroom. There was a white cabinet, with painted gold trim, and a white marble sink that had thick black veins running through.

Laura bent over and opened the cabinet, pulling out a 40 pack of tampons and set them on the counter. Like it was nothing. After she retrieved an individually wrapped cylinder, she tore the tissue off like she was peeling a banana.

"So you stick this inside you," Laura said.

"Won't it hurt?"

"No, silly." She patted the sink. "Sit up here and I'll walk you through it."

It was all so strange sitting on the edge of her sink, with my legs spread open. But I was desperate and wanted to know how to plug up the blood. Laura handed me the opened tampon.

"Okay, push this in," she said.

I tried to find the hole, but it was awkward.

"Are you sure it'll fit?"

"You're missing it," Laura said, bending over watching me.

I jabbed and jabbed around my crotch until I found the slick entrance, and finally, the cardboard tube easily slid in. I pushed the outer cardboard and the wad of cotton was left inside me.

"That wasn't so hard, was it?" Laura asked, as I slide off the sink.

"I will give you a few more but you're going to have to ask your dad to buy you your own."

The thought of asking my Dad horrified me, but buying them myself, horrified me even more. I would end up asking my Dad.

*

My entire family loved the annual pyrotechnics show at the Santa Monica pier. But we also indulged in our own fireworks display every 4th of July that included Roman candles, bottle rockets, and sparklers, with the other neighborhood kids. Dad would dangle a cigarette from the corner of his mouth and use it to light each fuse. He got such a kick out of our ooh's and ahhh's when the fiery sparks whipped across the night sky in an arc and the gasps of kids when there was a loud sudden bang. Some of the greatest joy I ever saw on my dad's face was when we'd laugh or scream after he'd blow something up.

At thirteen, I had inherited my dad's love for fireworks, so when he handed me a grip of firecrackers, laced together by fuses and a Zippo lighter, I felt as if it was another rite of passage.

"These are for me?" I stared down as he gently placed them in my outstretched palms like they were something holy. This meant thrills for whoever I recruited to join me in the fun, which of course turned out to be Laura.

"I think you're old enough now, just make sure you give yourself plenty of time after you light the fuse." Good, solid fatherly advice. "And light them in an alley."

While fireworks were legal at the time, we both knew that they were supposed to be done with adult supervision.

"Thanks Dad," I said, grabbing him around the neck and planted a kiss on his cheek.

*

The next day Laura and I met at a corner a few blocks from my house.

"How many did you get?" she asked. Her blond bangs looked like they had been meticulously cut by a surgeon, but I knew they had been done by her doting mom.

I held out the firecrackers in one hand and the Zippo in the other.

"Your dad is so frigging cool," she said, gushing.

"Right! Who knew?"

The houses in that section of Santa Monica had alleys where all the trash bins were to keep the palm-tree lined streets looking pristine, as if the houses there produced no waste. We picked one of the deserted alleys and made our way down to the middle. When we were well off the street, we huddled together, smiling as we unraveled the fuses. The adrenaline was already pumping through my veins.

Carefully untying each fuse, I handed the lighter to Laura. "You go first."

"Get ready to run as fast as you can," she said.

Carefully, she snapped open the Zippo and flicked it with her thumb, igniting the blue-orange flame to ignite.

"You ready?"

"Yes. Do it. Do it."

"Okay, here goes." She lit the fuse and threw it with an underhand pass.

Laughing, we both ran away. I jumped when I heard the bang behind us.

"That was so much fun," Laura said. "Now, it's your turn." She handed me the lighter.

I was smiling as I pulled out one of the firecrackers from my shirt pocket. I looked up at Laura right before I lit it. "Run, run, run," I said.

We both screamed and ran in the other direction. When we heard another loud bang, we cracked up so much, I had to bend over and hold my thighs.

"Oh my god. That one was even louder!" I said.

We must have fired off a dozen of them. The smell of gunpowder and Sulphur hung in the air. All of a sudden, at the opposite end of the alley, I saw an unmarked police car roll to a stop.

"Oh shit," I said.

"What?"

"That's a narc car," I said.

"Run!" she yelled. We both turned and ran in the other direction.

When we got to the end of the alley, Laura yelled, "Split up."

We ran in different directions. My plan was to run home and I'm sure Laura was going to do the same thing. My legs and arms were pumping, but just as I got to the intersection the narc car skidded to a stop directly in front of me.

A woman with a short bob haircut hopped out and yelled, "Police! Stop right there!" She pointed at me like I was a criminal.

What choice did I have but to freeze?

The woman stormed over and got inches from my face. "What's your name, young lady?"

"Why? What's the matter?" I said, feigning innocence.

"Shooting fireworks is illegal within city limits."

"It is? I didn't know."

"What's your name?"

"Wendy."

"Who was your friend?"

"Just some kid... I don't know.."

We all knew that you don't snitch on your friends.

"Oh, so you want to play that game, do ya?" She grabbed me back of the arm and led me to her car. "Then you're going down to the station."

When we got to the car, the officer put a hand on my head to guide me into the back seat. I thought she was making such a big deal about the fireworks. It wasn't all that necessary. I had no idea this would not be my last time pressed in the back seat of a police car.

I wasn't too worried because I had seen enough television to know I had the right to make one phone call at the station. Once I got him on the phone, Dad would explain the fireworks, and then she'd have to let me go.

The officer stepped on the gas. Whenever the car turned a corner, I slid across the leather seat and my shoulder would slam into the door. My thoughts were doing the same thing. Ten minutes later we were pulling into a lot where she parked in front of a squat building. The officer came around and once again grabbed me by the back of my arm and led me up a narrow stairwell that emptied onto a long hallway with a beehive of uniformed cops everywhere. Some of them nodded when they saw her. "Hey Morgan, got a collar," one officer said.

"Yeah, we got ourselves a wanna-be tough girl here," she said.

Everyone was acting like I was some sort of felony bank robber or something. It was only firecrackers, people! Lighten the fuck up.

On the door of her office was a sign that read, Detective Morgan, Juvenile Division.

"Have a seat." Morgan pointed as she moved behind her desk.

Morgan stared me down, and even though I knew this was an intimidation technique, it was working. With my eyes cast down, I studied the ragged cuticles on my hands. My ribcage was vibrating.

"I'm going to ask you again, who was your friend?" Morgan said.

"I don't know her name."

"So, you play with kids that you don't know?"

"Sometimes..."

Morgan slammed down both hands on her desk. "That's it, Missy! If you don't come clean, I'm going to throw the book at you."

"For fireworks?"

I didn't understand what the big deal was, Morgan was acting like I had committed a murder or something. My palms were all sweaty. My heart thumped inside my chest. I shifted in the hard chair as Morgan went to the door, and yelled at one of the lower ranking officers.

"Hey Brooks, come take this smart ass to a cell."

"Can I get my one phone call please?"

"You got nothing coming!"

A rookie with a crew-cut appeared.

"Cuff her," Morgan said.

"You don't need to cuff me. I'm not going to run."

"Put your hands behind your back," he said, unsnapping his leather pouch.

The hand cuffs tightened around my wrists like painful bracelets.

"Put her in one of the female adult cells," Morgan said.

"Sure thing," he said, leading me by the back of my arm.

As I was led down a brightly lit corridor, uniformed cops stopped what they were doing to glare at me. I was led down another stairwell to the booking department which felt like a dungeon. The rookie took me down a long hallway and through two heavy doors to the back, to a cell where he uncuffed me from behind.

"Get in," he said.

Stepping inside, I jumped when he slammed the gate behind me. I examined the six by seven-foot cell that had two metal bunks hinged to a cinder block wall. There was a stainless-steel toilet and a sink in the corner. I sat down on the thin vinyl mattress and cupped my forehead inside my hands. If she was trying to scare me, it had worked. I was terrified.

Seconds, minutes, hours ticked by, as I lay on the bunk. Tears filled my eyes and I tried to push them back down, convincing myself it would soon be all over.

Surely, my dad would give these assholes a good what for-, for treating his daughter like this. You just wait, Morgan. You're going to be so sorry you did this to me.

I couldn't hold back the tears any longer. It was the end of the day when Brooks finally came back to let me out. This time I wasn't handcuffed. When I saw the back of my dad's head in Morgan's office, I was convinced that he had already set her straight.

"Have a seat, Wendy," Morgan said.

I sat down next to my father.

"Your father and I have had a nice little chat." She smiled.

He interrupted her. "I want you to tell the detective who you were with."

"But, I, but...."

The walls of the room seemed to close in on me. I knew he wanted me to give Laura up, but not to tell on him. Dad was always invested in how he looked to authority. I knew if I exposed him for the culprit who gave me the fireworks he'd be pissed off at me.

"Did you hear me?" he leaned closer. "Who was it?"

"I was with Laura." The words rolled right off my tongue.

Clearly, you would never ever want to drop me behind enemy lines.

Dad and Morgan gave each other a look, like not only were they in cahoots, but they were pleased that they had made the clueless teen cave in. Humiliation slithered up my spine.

"Alright Missy, you're free to go now," Morgan said. "But no more fireworks. You hear me?"

"Yes ma'am."

As a minor I'm sure it wasn't legal to handcuff me or throw me into a jail cell, but I would later come to understand what many law-abiding citizens don't understand. Many cops have their own code, and it teeters on the edge of the ones breaking the law. My encounter with Morgan was an introduction to an unjust justice system. And as bad as it might have seemed at the time, I'm convinced if I had darker skin and wasn't from privilege, it would have been even worse.

A few minutes later I was getting into Dad's car. He lit a cigarette. Gray smoke and anger fill the space between us. I lean my shoulder into the door as far away from him as I can possibly get. I'm cursing him out. He has betrayed me. In my mind I'm beginning to see him as a hypocrite trying to present the best version of himself to the world, even if it means that his daughter gets treated unjustly. My jaw was tight. I had to ask.

"Why didn't you say that you gave me the firecrackers?" I didn't wait for his answer. "You're just pissed that I got caught."

There are certain times when you hit so close to the truth, the other person doesn't know what to say. This was one of those times.

*

I was in 1st grade when I experienced my first crush on an older boy in the 5th grade. Every day I watched him playing basketball on the yard at recess. Shamelessly, I would stare in my pleated skirt and crisp white blouse, as he ran back and forth across the asphalt court. If the ball accidentally got knocked out of the court, I would retrieve it and throw it back to The Crush. At first he'd give me a smile with his perfect teeth and mouth, freckles splattered across his nose. My heart would flutter like the wings of a humming bird.

My obsession consumed me, but by month two, The Crush sent a wave of shock through my tiny six-year-old body when he yelled at me to go away.

I didn't know what to say or do. Had I done something wrong? If he would just tell me what I had done, I would have changed everything to get him to like me again. Confused, I found myself in tears in the girls' bathroom staring at my black and white Oxfords shoes.

By thirteen years old, I was much more mature having experienced dozens of infatuations. I had fallen in and out of love hundreds of times. I was accustomed to juggling one or two crushes simultaneously. In my mind's eye I had seen myself getting kissed, engaged and growing old with each of the boys I liked. Only none of them knew I was obsessed with them. All of it happened in my mind.

Fantasy had to be my first addiction. It took me away from my own life. As a kid when my mother was having one of her many breakdowns, I could conjure up a great white stallion who would gallop in and take me far, far away. In a classroom when I was bored to death, I could see myself at the beach on a hot day diving into the waves.

But when my latest crush, Matthew, actually approached me in the school yard with his curly brown hair hanging in his eyes, it was all new and foreign to me. "Want to meet after school?" he said.

"Ah... sure. Where?" I nervously twisted a strand of hair between my fingers.

"Let's meet in front of the church," he said, swaggering off.

It was hard to get through the rest of the day. All I thought about was the most popular boy in school asked me to meet him. And when the 3:00 bell finally rung I rushed out to the front of St. Monica's church. Matthew was sitting on the steps and it felt like all the angels had conspired to bring us together. Someone else might call it fate, I called it divine destiny. I believed it would take a boy like Matthew to fill the emptiness I carried inside. He would be the boy that would make me feel alright.

Dressed in my uniform, books tucked under my arm we walked off into the sunset. Only, a few minutes later my knight in shining armor was taking me into a parking structure nearby the school. Deep down in this dark dungeon, my heart was pounding inside my chest. I was having my first love affair in the real world. In my flesh. I had heard about French kissing from girlfriends, so I wanted to see what tongue on tongue would feel like.

Matthew led me behind a parked car and told me to sit on the cold, hard ground. And I did even though the air smelled of motor oil and disinfectant. Silently, Mathew sat next to me and put his hand under my starched crisp blouse. For a moment I was embarrassed that he was rubbing my flat chest, and I wanted to tell him to stop. But when the tips of his fingers crept under my pleated blue skirt, the breath got stuck in my throat. His fingers made their way inside me, and I must have shuddered a hundred tremors into his hand.

There were two things going on in that moment. I felt deep shame for participating in such a dirty act that the nuns would classify a mortal sin, but I loved the feeling of being touched inside a private place where no one else had ever been. How can something that feels so good make me feel so bad at the same time? I had no idea.

I watched Matthews blue eyes, wide open as they were and the way he chewed on his lower lip. I was doing my best to convince myself that he was in love with me.

We never did French kiss. We didn't kiss at all. And when it was all over Matthew said, "See ya tomorrow," and he walked away.

Later, that night I fantasized about Mathew asking me to go steady with him. I imagined us going to the movies, to the beach and the two of us becoming an item at school. But the next day when I walked down the corridor, I noticed kids whispering as I passed by. I knew Matthew had told all his friends. And as rumors spread through the school like wildfire, the shame and self-hatred coiled up in my belly.

I wanted to die. Again.

*

After Matthew, I hated my school even more. I hated the frumpy uniforms, the daily prayers, and confessions to the priests. Most of all, I hated the nuns. In my mind, I ranked each of them using a metric of hatred, factoring in their level of cruelty. On the top of that list, by a remarkable margin, was Sister Mary Magdalena. Every day I would sit in the classroom and watch her black silhouette as she continuously tapped a nub of chalk spewing out world history. For a kid whose only interest was sneaking cigarettes in the school bathroom, the lessons seemed pointless as I drifted somewhere inside my head. But when she'd scream or slap the palm of her hand against her desk it got everybody's attention. Even mine.

"Listen up!" she'd yell. "I will be asking these questions in the exam so pay attention..."

I thought the lessons she taught would never be used in real life because I had no idea what an education was actually for. I didn't know that there was a base knowledge I would need to be granted access to a wider world. What does it matter what wars were fought centuries ago, how treaties were signed and who the dead presidents were? It all seemed like such a waste of time back then.

One day, I was writing a note to a friend asking if she wanted to hang out after school when Sister Magdalena saw me.

"Wendy, what are you doing there?" she demanded.

"Um-taking notes."

"Put that away right now!"

"Alright. Alright..." I said, pushing the paper under my notebook.

With her brow crunched, Sister Magdalena turned to continue her lessons on the blackboard. A cartoon of defiance, I stuck my thumbs in my ears and wiggled my fingers behind her back. While sometimes I wanted to disappear, there were times I insisted on being seen. Some of the others couldn't help but crack up laughing. Sister Magdalena spun around, her veil swirling like black wings ready to reach their full span. It looked as if she might actually take off like the Flying Nun. Immediately, her gaze landed on me. Feigning innocence, I raised my hands in the air. She glared at me, assessing, ready to strike but since she couldn't prove anything, she turned back to the board.

This time, I started making clicking noises with my tongue which caused another round of laughter. Sister Magdalena came rushing down the aisle and stopped at my desk, standing above me, nostrils flared.

"Why are you making those sounds?"

"What sounds?"

"Clicking your tongue."

"I wasn't clicking my tongue."

Her mouth was pulled tight on her pale face that had probably never been exposed to any sun. There was a mere slit where her lips should have been.

"Go sit in the corner." She pointed at the chair in the back of the room designated for unruly kids.

"But why? I didn't do anything."

"Just do it!"

I got up and walked over, plopping myself down in the small chair. Sister Magdalena followed close behind me.

"Look straight ahead," she said, pointing toward the wall. "And don't turn around."

After years of housekeepers who would lie to us, rob from us or get drunk with my dad, my response to authority figures was to do exactly the opposite of what they said. I glared at her, gaze steady, the challenge of a child. Sister Magdalena was swift with her response, a clean slap across my face. My cheek burned. Immediately, I wanted to cry, tears springing up with the insistent sting, but I refused her the satisfaction. Instead, I smiled back at her. I wondered when the last time was that I smiled at an adult with any earnestness at all.

Sister Mary Magdalena's face turned a blotchy red as she raised her arm up and slapped me again, same cheek, same burn.

"Don't turn around," she said. Spit spewed out of her mouth as she spoke.

All I could do was smile even wider this time.

That was enough to send Sister Magdalena over the edge. She raised her hand and slapped me again. And then again, over and over. With each blow, my head spun with the impact. I packed all the shock, all the pain, all the humiliation and I swallowed it down.

Don't cry, I told myself.

I can only imagine the horror of the other students as they watched. Watched their teacher completely lose her shit. I heard gasps. Whispers too, but none of that registered as she tried her best to break me down.

I would not shed one fucking tear.

Do not cry!

Self-preservation was a skill I had inadvertently learned growing up with a mother who was constantly trying to kill herself. It came from armoring up against a father's sarcasm as well. Over time, any doors that opened to astonishment and wonder were gone. I had become more than flesh and bone. I was filaments of anguish, nerve-endings of disappointment with a trigger-finger, locked, loaded and ready to shoot. My days of praying for any God to help me were over. I was my mother's ghost. I was as solid as any brick wall.

When Sister Magdalena finally stopped slapping me and went back to the front of the room, she was completely out of breath. My cheek was on fire as I stared at a shaft of light coming in from a window making a square on the linoleum floor. My breath was shallow, my jaw pulled tight. Energy was pulsing throughout my entire body, but I didn't budge. The other students stayed just as still. While I may have appeared calm, my mind was thrashing with thoughts of payback. Dogshit in her desk drawer. Hide the chalk so she'd never teach again. Or better yet, stop showing up to her class entirely. That would show her. But one thing for sure, Sister Magdalena may have humiliated me, left her mark across my face, but she did end up teaching me one lasting lesson, which was never let anyone see your tears.

It stuck. No one would make me cry for many years to come.

*

It was the summer of '66 and the Vietnam war protests were in full swing. Martin Luther King Junior had been struck in the head with a rock by a crowd of angry white men during a march in Chicago. But here in sunny, Southern California, I was upset that I had to attend summer school when I'd much rather be spending my days riding horses at Crestwood Stables. Life was so unfair.

One day, instead of going to school I took a bus to the stables. It was located on the ridges of the Santa Monica Mountains. My friend, Mary Jo, and the rest of the kids that hung out there owned their own horses. My dad said we couldn't afford to buy me one–though I did ask. Over time, I had made friends with the owner. Janet was a woman who seemed as if she were plucked straight out of the old frontier. She had a long brown ponytail, boots with a hollow thump, and leather chaps with the crotch area cut-out. She looked like a cowgirl who could milk a cow, lasso a calf and brand cattle all by herself.

Coming up the dirt path, I saw Rory, a sixteen-year-old stunt rider. He was looping around on his black steed inside the corral. He dipped down around the horse's chest and came up the other side in one sweeping movement. Rory was a cutie-pie with thick dark hair. He was focused on working in Hollywood and barely talked to anyone, but just the same, I could watch him ride for hours.

As I got closer to the office, customers were clustered around waiting for horses. Fly strips spiraled down along the edge of the rafters with dead flies stuck all over the sticky paper. Bales of hay sat stacked next to the office door with two young girls perched on top of them. The sign-in sheet on the clipboard was damn-near full. A rental horse was $1.50 an hour back then, but most people went out for two hours so they had more time to enjoy the trail.

"You need some help, Janet?" I called.

Janet looked up. "That would be great, Wendy. Will you get me Buttercup?"

"Yes ma'am."

The horses were kept in a pen beyond a tall swinging gate. Part of the pen was covered with a canopy where horses lined up for hay in a long trough at feeding time. I grabbed a halter from the tack room where bridles and ropes rested on hooks.

Ever since I was a child, I had a deep love for everything equestrian. It might have been from all those hours I sat in front of a television set watching *Bonanza* and *Rawhide* with my Dad or reading books like *Black Beauty*, but somehow I knew what to look for in the horse's body language when I interacted with them. I knew if the ears were fully back and down, it was important to stay clear of their hind quarters in case they kicked. If their ears swiveled that might mean they were anxious and trying to gauge the location of the approaching human. The upright ears usually meant the horse was content. Ears pointing forward meant receptivity–without fear. This interest and awareness for the subtleties of the horses I just couldn't muster for my own schoolwork.

I didn't have to worry about Buttercup though, the gentle golden Palomino who stood about 15 hands high. I knew Buttercup because I had ridden her for over a year, until Janet suggested I try a more challenging horse.

Once I got Buttercup in my sights, I followed her until she backed into a corner.

"Come on, girl. Time to get some exercise." I ran my hand up her haunches, across her muscular back. Standing by her neck, I slipped on the harness, and led her to the tack room where I tied her to a post.

"It's okay, girl," I whispered. I grabbed a brush, giving her short swift strokes shaking dust from her coat. Then I threw a blue pad on her back and a western saddle over that. I reached underneath her chest and grabbed the leather strap, cinching it into a silver metal ring. After replacing the halter with a bridle, I led Buttercup out front.

"Is that my horse?" A little girl with pig-tails jumped up and down. I laughed at her excitement, recognizing myself.

"That's yours, alright," Janet said.

The morning rush hours were the busiest time at the stables. That's when everyone wanted to ride. After helping Janet for several hours my reward was taking one of the horses out on the trail myself. At the time I was riding Midnight, a lean compact mix of Arabian/ Quarter horse. When I approached Midnight, his ears stood erect. I like to think she was glad to see me as I put her halter on, her long mane hanging down past her neck.

I always rode bareback because it felt more natural. I didn't want a cumbersome saddle coming between me and the horse. After I brushed Midnight coat, I leaped on her back and sat up straight. With the bridle gripped in my hand I went to look for Mary Jo. I found her bent over her black and white pinto cleaning his hooves with her fine brown hair framing her narrow face.

"Hi Mary Jo," I said, outside the stall.

"Oh hey."

"Can you go out?"

"Hold on, Lady's almost ready."

A few minutes later Mary Jo and I were heading out on the trail side by side. We talked about boys, horses and whatever teens talked about back then. The bright sun cut through patches of clouds that drifted across the sky like a flock of sheep. Once past the upper corral it was time to pick up speed. I grabbed a handful of Midnight's mane and we let our horses go. As their hooves hit the ground, a wave of dust rose in the air behind us. I could feel the muscles in Midnight's back tensing as my calves gripped his chest. Whenever I gave

Midnight full reign, he had the absolute determination
to be out in front. Galloping at a fast speed made me
feel like I was flying. It made me forget about summer
school. Forget about my fucked up home life. About
the awkwardness of being in my body. It made me feel
like I was free.

Two hours zipped by, and when Mary Jo and I got
back to the stable we brushed our horses before we put
them away for the day.

A few minutes later we walked to the parking lot
where a bunch of stable kids were passing around a
cigarette. I don't know how long we were talking with
them when my dad pulled up in his shiny new car. My
heart pounded inside my chest as the passenger window went down. "Get over here, Wendy!" he yelled, his
lips pulled tight.

"Uh, oh. Looks like you're in trouble," Mary Jo said.

I bit my lower lip and walked towards him.

"You ditched school today!" he said, as I climbed in
the front seat.

In the set of his jaw and the vacuum of his gaze I saw
something very close to disgust. All of a sudden, his
hand reached up in a single coiled-spring motion, and
he slapped me. The sting made me grab for my face. I
felt my throat close up.

He hit the gas pedal hard. When I turned to look
at Mary Jo and the rest of the kids, they were staring
at me. The taste of shame rose up in the back of my
throat. I lowered my head.

As a teenage girl, every emotion, humiliation or disappointment seemed magnified under a high-powered

telescope. I shrank inside and made a decision never to go back to the stables because I couldn't face those people ever again. And I never did. Over time, I would convince myself the freedom I had while on the back of a horse was just another thing my father took from me.

*

It's a wonder that Laura and I were still friends after I told Detective Morgan that she was the one shooting firecrackers with me. But after giving me shit for 'snitching,' Laura got over it fairly quick. One hot summer day when I was thirteen, Laura and I were making our way down the creaky, musty planks of the Santa Monica pier. Laura had thick white calves and ankles that stretched out below her girly summer shift. I had on frayed cut offs, a halter top and flip flops. We stopped at the carousel to watch it go around and around. The organ music swallowed us up in a breathless cloud of sound. A wide-eyed girl with pigtails flapping in the wind rode by on brightly painted wooden stallion while I lit up my cigarette.

"Want one?" I offered Laura my pack.

"Sure." Her blonde hair framed her face as she struck the match.

I had started smoking. Maybe I was already hooked on nicotine from inhaling second-hand smoke growing up. Dad almost always had a cigarette between his fingers or hanging from the corner of his mouth. Or maybe it was those bubble gum cigarettes I bought from the ice cream man, but somehow, I concluded that smoking was the thing to do. After all, everyone in the movies did it. I remember studying intently women who smoked on screen. The elegant actresses holding a cigarette between their fingers, bringing it to their pouting mouths before blowing the smoke into the leading man's face. Or even better, the contempt on Betty Davis's face as she glared through thick, black lashes, giving the world a huge fuck you every time she took a puff. Smoking was a prop that could define who you were in the world. At thirteen it made me look and feel older, and as a teen that was something I was desperately trying to achieve.

We walked down the pier passing the ring-toss booths with the stuffed animals lined up in the back. When we got to the shooting booth, a mustached man with a belly hanging over his belt had an air rifle squinting with one eye. Ducks popped up and down with painted tin birds flying by on an assembly line. He pulled the trigger and a 'pop' pierced the air. When he missed the target, profanity came spilling out of his mustached mouth. Laura and I looked at each other and laughed. He must have heard us because he turned around and pierced us with his blue dagger eyes. We laughed and ran off down the pier.

We were no longer interested in carnival games. We preferred hanging out in the arcade, a huge building divided by pinball machines, photo-booths, and a juke box on one side and pool tables on the other.

Ever since I had watched Minnesota Fats with my dad, I was obsessed with the game of pool. Balls rushing across green felt, clicking against each other gave me goose bumps. But in order to play, you'd have to challenge somebody on one of the tables by setting a single quarter down. My eyes landed on Sam, a tall, lanky Black dude who could empty the entire table with one shot after another. I tried to play with Sam whenever I could, to learn the tricks of the trade. Laura headed off to pose in the picture booth, while I laid a quarter down on Sam's game.

"So, you looking to play?" Sam asked.

"If you don't mind playing with an amateur?" I tucked my hands into the pockets of my shorts.

"You kidding girl? Get yourself a stick."

I hunted for the perfect cue-stick in the racks against the wall. I found one that looked good and extended it like an arrow, squinting with one eye to make sure it wasn't crooked. It looked straight so I chalked the tip so it wouldn't slip when I hit the cue ball.

I dropped a quarter into the slot and the balls released, clicking into one another. I scooped the balls up and dropped them into the wooden triangle rack. Sam squinted one eye and made a bridge with his double-jointed thumb so he could thrust the stick into the cue ball causing all the balls to fan out over the green felt.

"Wow! What a break," I said.

"If you look at this, Wendy, it actually sets you up for a shot."

I followed his gaze to a red-striped ball not far from corner pocket. I leaned over, strategizing my shot.

"Hit the ball slightly to the left of center." Sam came up behind me.

"Like this?" I moved the tip of the cue slightly.

"Yup. That's it." Sam was practically spooning me now, but I didn't say anything. No one ever told me I could tell someone to stop doing something I didn't like. Even if I would have had the words back then, I wouldn't have used them because I wanted everyone to like me.

When Sam stepped away, I pulled my elbow back and with one quick jab, sent the cue ball spinning toward its target. The red ball plopped into the side pocket.

"I did it!"

"Well done champ."

Then I noticed Sal, a guy who hung around a lot in the arcade, dressed in a t-shirt and khakis. My body exploded with desire. A desire I didn't understand.

"Earth to Wendy," Sam said, tapping his cue stick against the floor. "It's your shot."

"Oh yeah. Sorry."

Sam eyed my line of vision. "You know that guy is bad news, don't you?" Sam knew all the regulars.

"Why is that?"

"Trust me. I just know."

Even then I always gravitated towards the bad-ass boys. On a base level, I was afraid to be in the world, and I wanted someone to protect me. Someone to make me feel safe.

I lined up the next shot, but it was hard to focus. My attention was split. My eyes kept drifting toward Sal. I longed to talk to him but didn't know how.

After finishing the game, Sam hugged me, his hands lingering. It made me uncomfortable, but still not enough to say anything.

I positioned myself in the corner and lit up a cigarette. I took in a deep inhale puffing out my chest, all the while wishing Sal would see me from across the room and be struck by how cool I was. I thought if I stood a certain way or pulled on the cigarette like Betty Davis, I would finally get the guy, and maybe then, the feeling of being unlovable would disappear. Sal never did look my way but even if he had, it wouldn't have been enough to make that deep-rooted feeling of being unlovable go away.

Machete

My brother's silhouette hovered in the doorway of his room. Jay was seventeen and had a machete in his hand. The blade was a dark gray. He gripped it so hard his knuckles had gone bone-white. Dad stood behind a round ceramic table thirty feet in front of him. Diane and I were watching huddled together at the other side of the playroom. Just beyond us there was a sliding glass door that let out to the pool. If we'd been like other families, we might have been swimming away our afternoon until our eyes burned of chlorine.

"You better stay out of my room," Jay yelled.

"This is my house! I can go wherever I damn well please," Dad said.

"If you come in here again, I swear I'll kill you." Jay raised the tip of machete toward the ceiling. I thought he was going to fling it across the room.

"Okay. That's it. I'm calling the police." Dad turned so fast he almost lost his balance. Jay slammed his door, the lock engaging behind him. I followed Diane up the two steps into the hallway just outside his dark, cavernous room. Dad was sitting on his wooden swivel chair in front of his desk, the receiver of the phone held to his ear waiting for the police dispatcher to come on.

For the first seven years of my life, Mom and Dad's fights caused voices to echo off the walls. After Mom died it had gotten quiet for a while except for the normal bickering's of spoilt, unruly kids. Now, us kids were the ones who were doing the fighting, mostly with Dad.

Irene came rushing down the hall behind us. "Girls, girls, let your dad have some privacy," she said.

"If someone is getting chopped up with a machete I want to know," I said.

"Oh hush, silly, no one is getting chopped up." Irene was not convincing at all.

Reluctantly, Diane and I made our way to the living room where we plopped down on the sofa to get a better view of the unfolding drama.

"Do you think the cops will take him away this time?" I asked.

"They didn't when he tried to burn the house down," Diane said.

A few months before this Dad had smelled smoke coming from Jay's room. When he knocked on Jay's door he didn't answer, so Dad called the fire department. The fireman forced the door open and extinguished a pile of smoldering underwear in the center of his room. After a long lecture on the dangers of starting fires inside any structure, Jay said he'd never do it again.

Just a few years before this, Dad had been so proud of Jay's ability to maintain straight-As in school. But Jay, four years my senior, had always scared me. He had a trigger temper that could go off when you least expected. Like that time he punched me in the stomach for no apparent reason when we were playing in the back yard. When trying to describe his coming apart I can't pinpoint the one thing that sent him over the edge. His insanity was more like a slow, creeping thing. It was a rising tide, and by the time he was a teenager, the whole family was drowning under his rage. Dad seemed to have one tool only in his parenting arsenal: call the cops or the fire department. Let them deal with it.

A few minutes into this episode, the doorbell rang. My sister and I were pretending to watch television, but the entertainment in our own house was more gripping. When Dad answered the door two uniformed cops from the Santa Monica Police Department stood there. I recognized the one with a shock of white hair from another time Dad called the cops.

"Hello, Mr. Adamson," he said. "How can we help you?"

"My son just pulled a machete on me." Dad raised his hands up to the air. His round belly falling over his drawstring pajamas.

"Is this your son Jay, again?" The officer rested a hand on his revolver.

"Yes, yes, it's Jay again." Dad leaned sideways favoring his good leg.

"Can you tell us what happened?"

"He's angry because I went in his room. I thought he might be smoking marijuana and I don't tolerate that kind of thing in my home."

"Where is he now, Mr. Adamson?"

"Locked in his room," Dad pointed.

"Let us have a little talk with him."

The younger officer had blotchy, pink skin, and a blond crew cut. He tilted his head to look past my dad's shoulder at us. I slumped down and averted my eyes.

After my first encounter with police for shooting fire-crackers, I had a deeply ingrained disdain for all cops.

They followed Dad a quarter way down the hall, leather holsters creaking and handcuffs and keys jingling.

Dad knocked. "Jay, the police are here. They want to talk to you."

Silence.

"Let me try Mr. Adamson." The older Sargent knocked. "Jay? It's Sargent Murphy. Open up the door. We just want to have a talk."

Jay opened his door several inches.

"Can we come in?" the Sargent asked.

Jay let them in and they closed the door behind them. Dad went to the bar and made himself a vodka on the rocks and sat down in the living room with us.

"What's going to happen to Jay?" Diane asked.

"We'll have to see what the police say."

For some reason, Dad always looked up to authority figures. Maybe, as a widower with four, unruly children he was in over his head. Twenty minutes later the officers came back out.

"I don't think you have anything to worry about, Mr. Adamson. Jay has calmed down."

"Are you sure?"

"Yes Mr. Adamson, but I'd lock this up if I were you." He held out the handle of the machete. The gray steel blade looked less threatening with the officer holding it in his hand.

Just the same, it would take more than locking up the machete for me to feel safe. Less than a year later,

Jay, like Mom, would be diagnosed a paranoid schizophrenic. It turned out he suffered from delusions and
hallucinations that blurred the lines of reality, thus the
reason for his violent outbursts. It was evident that Dad
was unable to protect us and that's why he called the
cops all the time. Diane and I would become so terrified that Jay might chop us up to bits while we were
sleeping, that we took to propping up a chair against
our door every night before we went to bed. Fear was
my true north for many years to come.

Altered

Laura and I had made plans to get ready at her house for a party that was being held on the other side of Santa Monica. Laura lived on a cul de sac with manicured lawns and elaborate flower beds where all the houses oozed of privilege, with Mercedes Benzes and Cadillacs parked in the driveways.

I knocked on the door of the massive two-story house knowing her parents wouldn't be there because they had gone out. A few minutes later Laura answered the door wearing a tight black dress with yellow daisies printed across it. Laura had huge boobs that had started sprouting when she was twelve. While she claimed the size annoyed her, she certainly knew how to use those boobs to attract the attention of boys. This particular night, they threatened to burst right through the front of the dress, a blossoming just as impressive as the daisies she was wearing.

"Cool dress, Laura." I made sure to enunciate my words, giving her the flattery that was needed by any insecure teen.

"You really like it?" Laura brushed her hands down the front of her body.

"Oh yeah. It's really cute!"

"I like your outfit, too," she said, with a nod. "Very Cher."

I had on skin-tight bell-bottom jeans, a crop-top and a faux leather jacket. A lot of preparation had gone into choosing this outfit, but I still felt insecure.

"Really? Not too casual?"

"Oh no. Not at all." Laura waved me into the foyer under a crystal chandelier. "Let's go upstairs," she said.

I followed Laura up the familiar spiral staircase to her bedroom. The clean, crisp smell of lemon filled the house. The maid had probably been there earlier that day. When we got to her room, Laura plopped down on a round stool in front of the vanity and leaned forward to admire herself in the mirror. I sat on the edge of the nearby bed and examined the expensive perfumes on the crystal tray she had obviously gotten from her mother. A familiar pang of jealousy rippled through me. The longing for a mother was always there, just under the surface. It could tug at my heart when I least expected it. But the jealousy was outweighed by the fear of going to the party that night.

For weeks I had been imagining myself walking into the party with confidence and greeted by friends who were actually happy to see me. But as the party grew closer my illusion started to fade. The truth was I didn't feel comfortable. I never felt comfortable. I was self-conscious beyond measure. Of course, I didn't mention these fears to anyone. They were too embarrassing to speak of. Instead, I made a plan to bring alcohol to see if that might help with my nervousness. I had never drunk alcohol before, but I knew teens who had, and I was ready to give it a try for myself. I pulled out the fifth of vodka I'd taken from Dad's bar and stuffed in my macramé purse earlier in the day. The red and silver Popov label was wrapped snuggly across the front. The clear liquid inside looked crisp and clean as a glass of water--so innocent. What harm could there be?

"Look what I got," I said, holding it up so Laura could see the reflection of the bottle in the mirror.

"Holy shit." She spun around on her dainty stool. "You brought the whole bottle?"

"Why not?" I shrugged.

Laura had bragged that her parents let her have a sip of wine in the past, so I figured she'd be totally down for it. I passed the bottle to her so she would go first.

Wide eyed, Laura carefully broke the seal and twisted off the cap. She hesitated only briefly before throwing it back, taking several large pulls. Immediately, she coughed causing those massive breasts to jiggle as she heaved.

"You okay?" I asked.

"That shit burns going down." She handed it back to me.

All the muscles in my body tensed as I brought the bottle up and kissed the rim with my cherry-flavored lip gloss. As I lifted it up, my long brown hair inched down my back. The warm alcohol moved swiftly down the back of my throat. Heat lit up my entire chest. Instantly, a calm washed over me. The logic seemed clear: if one drink made me feel that good, two drinks would make me feel even better. I took another swig. I was struck with a confidence that had been completely out-of-reach just moments before. Not only that, when I looked at my image in the mirror, I saw a different person staring back at me. My long brown hair looked silky, cascading over my shoulders. My blemishes completely disappeared. I looked pretty. Sexy, even. That had never happened before.

Shit, I was ready to go to that party now.

I don't remember how we got there, but there was already a beehive of activity with kids from my school, milling around in the driveway and in the back yard. Where I would normally fold in on myself, that night, I sashayed in fearless and bold. A string of white overhead lights illuminated the faces of the partygoers in a mysterious glow. I made my way to the table where an assortment of soda and chips were laid out. Scooping up some guacamole with a corn chip, I shoved it in my mouth, unashamed.

Laura wandered away from my side, beckoned by some boy. I didn't care that she'd left. I didn't care that I had dropped guacamole on my crop top. In that moment, all I wondered about was where was that groovy music coming from? I followed the sound up the back stairs to a rec room over the garage. Inside there was an orange lava lamp glowing in the corner. Posters of rock stars hung from the walls. A girl I barely knew waved at me. This was where all the cool, popular kids were hanging out—the kids that never talked to me at school. This was where I wanted to be. I plopped myself down in an oversized chair and closed my eyes to listen to Mick Jagger's voice thumping through the speakers. My head felt lighter with the absence of all the self-doubt I normally felt.

I was in the moment until I looked up and saw Jessie, one of the hottest guys in school walk in the door. He was wearing motorcycle boots and a leather jacket and his thick black hair was combed back. Usually, when I saw Jessie strutting down the school hallway, he'd send my heart fluttering like the wings of a bird. But we never actually talked, and he would only acknowledge me with a nod. On this particular night his blue eyes roamed my way. And then he smiled. Normally I would have been terrified, but under the magical spell of alcohol, I tilted my head sideways and smiled back.

Then something extraordinary happened. He walked towards me and sat down on the arm of the chair I was sitting in. My heart was pounding inside my chest. I looked up at him through black mascaraed lashes.

Typically, when I talked to a cute boy, words would get jumbled inside my mouth, but not that night. "How's it going Jessie?" I said.

"Getting better by the minute." Right away, he was flirting with me.

I twirled a strand of my long hair around my index finger.

"You look different somehow, Wendy."

"I do?"

"Yeah." The tip of his tongue swept over his upper lip. "You look really good."

Something stirred between my legs that forced me to press my thighs together. This was desire on a cellular level. Images flitted behind my eyes, seeing his heart-shaped lips against my mouth. With an unfamiliar boldness, I laid my hand on the muscles of his upper leg and leaned in towards his face.

All of a sudden, the room began to spin. I was looking at the world through a bowl of water. My vision doubled, watery traces. Sweat beaded up on my forehead. A guttural moan escaped my lips. All at once I leaned over and vomited everything in my stomach onto Jessie's cool black leather boots.

He leaped up. "What the fuck?"

I heaved again, and this time it was projectile-style clear across the room.

In an act of adolescent mercy, some girl in a tight mini-skirt sprang into action, and the next thing I knew, I was in a bathroom kneeling on the hard tile in front of the toilet. The mini-skirted girl disappeared while the mother of the house took her place. She held my hair and stroked my back in cooing circles.

I didn't fight it or move away. The sensation of being cared for by a woman was completely foreign to me. I don't remember much after that but Laura told me the next day that the mother drove me home, where I was quickly sent to my room by my dad.

When I woke up the next morning fully clothed, I had a headache. It felt like an entire army had marched through my mouth. My thoughts took me straight back to the party the night before.

Oh Shit! Jessie must think I'm such a loser. All the kids are going to be talking about me now.

As I laid there looking up at the cottage cheese ceiling I was mortified. But eventually my memory took me back to that first sip of when the vodka warmed my chest and filled me with relief. In the midst of a massive hangover, I had a revelation. Alcohol was what I had been looking for all my life.

I couldn't wait to drink again.

The Lie

Weeks after the party, I sat on the floor with my back against the side of my bed watching reruns of I Love Lucy. It was quiet. A rarity in my house. Dad was out on a date with his occasional girlfriend, Doris. I didn't like Doris much because she seemed like she was trying too hard. But I did like the fact that Dad was gone. All of a sudden Diane came bursting into the room, eyes rimmed with red, face flushed.

"Diane! What's wrong?"

"Irene wants to talk to you. She's in the dining room."

"Why? What happened?"

The laugh track on I Love Lucy went on and on. "Just go, Wendy," she said, gesturing toward the door.

I pushed myself up and made my way to the dining room where Irene sat at the table. The sun had just gone down and I could tell she was already buzzed by the faraway look on her face. Her pudgy fingers scissored a cigarette. When she took a puff, her lips almost covered the entire filter.

"Diane said you wanted to talk to me?"

"Sit down, Wendy."

I lowered myself in the chair across from her.

"I think it's time you know the truth about your mother." Irene sounded like she had marbles in her mouth when she had drank too much. "Your Dad's never going to tell you."

To hear her mention my mother made my stomach coil up in a knot. No one ever talked about my mother. There was an unspoken contract in which we didn't discuss her, and over time the memories had started to fade.

"What are you talking about, Irene?"

"Your mother committed suicide."

My entire body braced as the veil to Dad's deception was ripped away. I knew deep down that Irene was speaking the truth. Irene had been with us a couple of years by then, and over time she and Dad had become drinking buddies. They would stay up late, the sound of their voices and laughter often waking us up. Dad must have confessed things to Irene on one of those blurry nights, things he could not tell his children. Irene's disclosure answered so many questions for me. I had always wondered why Dad was uncomfortable whenever we brought up the subject of our mother. I wondered why we never went to her funeral. Why I never saw my maternal grandparents or cousins after her death. No wonder I had fantasies that she might be alive somewhere, and one day walk in the front door saying it all had been a big mistake.

As the fragments started to assemble in my mind, I wanted to confront Dad and demand the truth from him once and for all.

My jaw was clenched as I stared down Irene.

"If he's lied about mom what else has he lied about?" I asked.

"He was trying to protect you kids."

I stood up, almost sending the chair toppling behind me.

"Wait, Wendy..."

I stormed back to my room and found Diane laying on her bed.

"She told you?" Diane said, studying me.

I sat down on my bed. "It makes perfect sense now."

"Are you going to say something to Dad?" she asked.

"Hell, yeah. Aren't you?"

"What's the point?"

I couldn't believe she didn't get that Dad needed to be held accountable for his betrayal. "To let Dad know that he's a liar," I said.

"I've got my own plan and that's to get as far away from this bullshit as I can, just as soon as I turn 18." She only had a few more years to go before she could move out.

Diane was beyond confronting Dad, because she had a goal of going to nursing school and joining the Peace Corps after. And later, she would do both of those things while I would continue to let the rage eat me alive.

I fell backwards, head landing on my pillow, staring at the ceiling. Other than paying Dad back for his lies, I didn't have any goals of my own.

*

Dad didn't come home until late that night, and eventually, I fell asleep. But when I woke up the next morning, the first thing on my mind was confronting him. I stood in the doorway of his room barefoot, in pajamas. His king size bed was still unmade. His clothes from the night before were laid out over a chair. Old Spice and stinky cigarette smoke hung in the air. My heart was pounding inside my chest.

"Good morning," Dad said, lacing his brace around his polio-stricken leg.

"You lied to us about Mom."

He looked up at me. I had his complete attention now.

"Mom killed herself."

I heard him suck in a breath.

"Irene told you?"

"You lied to us."

"You were too young at the time."

Images came back to me in a rush—the day he told me Mom died of a heart attack, and then told me not to tell Bruce. The burden of that secret was a burden I couldn't hold alone.

"So that's why we didn't go to her funeral?"

I could almost see his chest deflate.

"You were only seven when it happened."

"Well, I'm fourteen now. When were you thinking of telling me?"

He took a moment, eyes gazing over my shoulder before he offers me up a weak excuse.

"I was waiting for the right time..." He held his palms up.

"When? When might have that been, Dad?" My voice echoed down the hall.

"I was just trying to protect you."

There was something that resembled defeat behind his eyes. Maybe he was so pummeled by the circumstances of his life that he had nothing more to give his kids. Maybe he thought he could buy us with material things like a beautiful home, a swimming pool and private schools.

"You were protecting us by lying?"

"You were too young to understand."

He did not say he was sorry. He never would.

He just sat there, shoulders slouched, looking pathetic. His hair was peppered with more gray than I recalled, his skin weathered from sun and time. A lot had happened since I was a little girl who used to tell him, I loves you all the time, Daddy. To think I used to curl up on his lap and feel safe. Irene even told me that I had been his favorite child. Well, it was obvious that would never be the same.

He was weak. A pathetic man. And I hated him for that.

After that day, the house was filled with even more ugliness. My rage became a black thing growing inside me. And over time, the blackness would take full reign of my life.

GIRLHOOD

Rebellion

I hung out with Tommy because at twenty-one he was old enough to purchase alcohol legally. At fourteen I had started to drink a lot. Sitting on the edge of Tommy's bed with my legs dangling over the side, I stared at the rotary phone on the nightstand. Tommy was in the living room watching television. I could hear the muffled sound of cartoons echoing down the hallway. In fact, I had passed out after drinking too much the night before and hadn't made it home. My stomach churned as I dialed my home number. My dad picked up on the first ring.

"Ah, hi Dad..."

"Where the hell were you last night?"

"I fell asleep at Laura's house and...."

"Don't give me that shit."

"But, but I did..."

"I spoke to Laura's mother and you weren't even there."

"But, I, I..."

"You fucking whore."

The words jabbed into my heart like needles. My jaw clenched so tight, it's a wonder my molars didn't turn to dust. I slammed down the phone and walked to the bathroom in a trance. The linoleum was sticky beneath my bare feet. A tube of toothpaste sat on the edge of the sink. I opened the medicine cabinet and picked up the double-edged razor I had seen while rifling through his cabinet the day before.

I brought it down fast, swiping it across my wrist like a credit card.

The debt had become due.

I cut at Dad.

I cut to punish him.

I cut to make him pay.

I cut because we were in some twisted power struggle. A warped chess game where no one could ever win.

There was a fleeting moment of satisfaction as I watched the flesh open up in a scream. Two rope-like tendons. A red ribbon of blood flowing from my wrist. But all of the sudden, I panicked and sweat beaded up on my forehead. My stomach coiled into a knot. There was way too much blood. My blood. A puddle was spreading out like black ink across the floor. I hadn't meant to cut so deep.

I turned and walked down the hall, extending my arm in front of me so I wouldn't get blood on my new 501 jeans. Tom & Jerry cartoons blasted from the television set. When Tommy looked up his mouth fell open. His eyes filled with horror.

"Fuck! What did you do?" He sprung up out of his recliner and led me back to the bathroom.

"Why? Why did you do this?"

"My dad pissed me off..."

"Your dad pissed you off?" He shook his head, a strand of oily hair falling in his face. "That makes absolutely no fucking sense."

He snapped a grimy towel from the rack and wrapped it around my wrist. Instantly bright red blood seeped through. "You're going to need stitches now."

"Can't we just put a butterfly band aid on it?"

"Are you crazy?"

Twenty minutes later Tommy's Chevy pulled up in front of Santa Monica Emergency Room. I held the useless towel on my arm. "They'll take care of you in there." He nodded toward the door.

"You're not coming with me?"

"Are you kidding? I can't go in." He shook his head fiercely. "You're a minor."

"Oh. Right...."

"Call me later and let me know how you're doing. Okay?"

"Yeah. Whatever."

As I watched Tommy drive away, I vowed never to call the stupid jerk again.

As I walked through the double doors, the emergency room was lit up like a Friday night football game. Several patients looked up as a gurney whirled by in a blur. Doctors' names and codes blared from the overhead PA system. My gaze landed on a woman sitting behind a desk with a heap of hair stacked on top her head. I walked over to her. "I think I might need stitches," I said, still holding the bloody towel.

"Oh, my goodness. What happened to you, sweetie?"

"Uh, I uh, had an accident."

"How old you are?"

"Fourteen."

"Well, I'm going to have to call your parents to get medical consent so we can treat you."

It never occurred to me that the hospital would have to call my dad. For some reason, I thought I would be patched up and be sent on my way. But I was impulsive. I hardly ever thought things through. Reluctantly, I gave her my home phone number. Maybe she'd have better luck talking to my Dad than I did.

"Alright sweetie, have a seat and the nurse will call you back in a minute."

As I sat on the hard plastic chair, I kept crossing and uncrossing my legs. A man with slumped shoulders was pacing back and forth. I didn't want to stare so I looked at the floor. Someone coughed behind me. I wanted to move far away from the germs being released into the air, but I didn't budge.

A few minutes passed before a young nurse with short brunette hair walked in. Her soft blue eyes studied me for a few seconds before calling me by my last name.

"That's me," I said, getting up.

She led me through the double doors in the back where separate cubicles were curtained off, each with an exam table inside.

"Climb on up," she said.

I used my good hand to get up as the nurse rolled over silver tray with instruments. Carefully, she unwrapped the bloody towel and tossed it in the trash. I looked down at her white laced up shoes with streaks of shoe polish running across the top. They reminded me of the oxfords I had to wear in Catholic school.

"What happened, sweetie?" she asked, dabbing the area with white gauze.

I let out an audible sigh. "I, um, cut myself."

"Why would you do that?"

"I was mad at my dad, and..."

Hearing myself, I realized just how stupid that sounded.

"You're much too young to do something like this," she said, stepping back and clasping her heart. "We all have problems with our parents. Every family is a mess. We just have to learn to live with it."

"No one has a family like mine," I said, shaking my head.

"You'd be surprised what some people endure."

At the time I was way too self-absorbed to think about other people in the world.

As the nurse cleaned up the blood and wrapped a piece of gauze around my wrist, I could see the precision of the razor cut.

"The doctor will be here in just a minute," she told me, her white shoes disappearing behind the curtain.

Afterward, I laid back on the table with my legs draped over the side. I tried to close my eyes, but the light was so bright it penetrated my eyelids. A beeping sound was coming from somewhere nearby. Probably machinery keeping someone alive. I was close to drifting off when the curtain slid open again and a good-looking doctor in blue scrubs came in. "Hello Wendy, I'm Doctor Mitchell." He set down the clipboard and took off the gauze the nurse had gently placed on my wrist. "I talked to your Dad. He's out in the lobby."

"You did? What did he say?"

"He's worried about you."

I knew he had talked to the public persona that my Dad used for people in a position of authority. Dad had another version just for me.

"You're going to need some stitches."

"Is it that bad?" I leaned in to get a closer look.

"You know, Wendy, I'm going to have to put you on a hold."

"What do you mean a hold?"

"The law says when anyone tries to kill themselves, we have to order a psychiatric evaluation."

"But I didn't really want to kill myself. I was just, just...."

He looked into my eyes waiting for my explanation, but I looked away.

"You'll be going to Camarillo State Hospital."

Shit. That was where they sent my mother.

"Camarillo is for crazy people." My voice quivered. "I'm not crazy."

"Well, normal people don't go around hurting themselves, Wendy."

In that moment I wanted to be normal more than anything else. I wanted a normal family like all the families on the television shows that I grew up watching as a kid. I wanted a mother, and I wanted a father who at least acted like he cared.

"This will hurt a little bit."

I flinched as the Novocain went into my wrist.

"Please let me go home, doctor. Please? I won't do it again. I promise."

"It's not up to me."

Squinting, the doctor meticulously pressed the edges of the wound together, then pushed the needle through one side of the skin to the other. With each stitch came a tug and a pull. My mind was racing with thoughts of regret. Why did you do this, you stupid girl? Why can't you just be like everyone else? What is wrong with you anyway? You're so stupid. When the doctor was done with my wrist it was zippered with short black threads, while my brain felt like it was unraveling.

"That should do it," he said, wrapping a long strip of gauze around my wrist several times. "Be careful not to put any strain on it and don't get it wet."

"Please let me go home, doctor?"

"I wish I could, but I hope you'll begin to see that you don't have to do this again." He smiled weakly and left.

After he was gone, I contemplated running. If I could get down the corridor and out the exit door before anyone grabbed me, I would go back to Tommy's and see if he would let me stay at his house.

Just then the curtain swept opened and Dad was standing there with his lips pulled tight and his red-tinged eyes glaring at me. I was ready to beg him to let me come back home, but before I could even utter a word, he looked at me with such disdain, and said, "Better luck next time."

My mouth dropped open. I felt like I had been sucker punched to the gut. I shifted on the gurney as he stomped off the other way and the curtain closed once again.

How could he say such a thing? He was my father, after all, and I was his daughter, even if I was a mess. At the time I had no words for my outrage, but even if I did, it was too late. The rage was taking on a life of its own, and it would find its own way out.

Institution Life

An ambulance took me in leather restraints on a gurney an hour up the coast. By the time I was admitted to the state hospital it was dark outside. The following morning, an intense throbbing in my wrist woke me up. Droplets of blood had seeped through the gauze. Regret swept over me. Again.

Kicking my feet out from under the wool blanket, I sat up on my bed. Behind me was a dorm with two rows of bunks beds and each with a tall metal lockers in between. A fluorescent light flickered on and off from above. I felt nauseous. What was that pill they had given me the night before? Whatever it was, I didn't like how it made me feel.

All of a sudden, a girl with a heap of disheveled red hair shuffled by. "You better hurry up if you want breakfast."

"Okay. Thanks," I said, grateful for any direction.

I got dizzy when I stood up. I had to hold onto the bunk. When my balance came back, and I was able to put on my street clothes that I came in with.

"Line it up for meds!" someone yelled from the doorway.

My thighs felt as heavy as lead and I had to force my feet to move. Taking one step at a time, I somehow managed to make it to the dayroom. Chairs had been lined up around the entire perimeter of a brightly lit room. A pool table sat just beneath the window of the nurse's station which was a fishbowl where staff could watch you at all times. A racoon-looking girl with dark circles under her eyes stared blankly off into space. A panic gripped my chest.

Holy shit! I don't belong here.

I approached the nurse's station where a doughy woman with moles dotting her face was giving out meds. She stood behind a Dutch door, the top half open, with a small shelf that held a pitcher of water and small paper cups. Behind her was another staff member who was scribbling inside a chart.

"Let me see your wristband," the nurse said.

I held out my arm with the white band with my name typed across it. The nurse's eyes squinted as she made out what it said, then she nodded. "You got in last night, Wendy, and the doctor ordered a little something for you." She held out a tiny cup with a tan coated pill inside.

"What is this?" I asked.

"Thorazine. It will help you relax."

At the time I had no idea what Thorazine was, but I wanted to be altered so I threw it in my mouth just the same. She handed me a tiny cup filled with water to wash it down.

"Just so you know, Wendy, breakfast is at seven, and you'll be seeing Dr. Kramer later today."

"Dr. Kramer?"

"He's the esteemed head psychiatrist here."

"Will he be the one to let me go home?"

She laughed and her neck jiggled like a bowl of Jell-O. "You'll have to ask him honey, but right now, you need to join the other girls." She pointed a red manicured finger toward a cluster of inmates who stood in front of a door.

This was a real deal mental hospital. It had heavy locked doors, cinder block walls, and bars on all the windows. How had I gone from my lifestyle in Santa Monica to this in just twenty-four hours? Holding onto a railing running along the wall of the corridor, I stood behind the rest of the girls. I felt the same kind of awkwardness whenever I was starting a new school. I didn't know what to do so I glared at the swirls on the recently-buffed linoleum floor. That's when I sensed someone was watching me. When I looked up, I met the gaze of a freckled-faced blond inmate several feet away. My internal armor went up. Was she the alpha-girl in this place, looking to fight?

She surprised me when her face lit up in a smile. Warily, I smiled back. She must have taken it as an invitation as she made her way through the other girls to stand directly in front of me. "Hi. My name is Patty," she said.

"Um. Hi. I'm Wendy."

"What brings you to this fine establishment of ours?"

Reluctantly, I showed her the bandage around my wrist.

"Oh hey, girl. I've done that before."

Patty extended a mutilated arm with white raised scars crisscrossing all the way up to her elbow. She clearly was a special authority on a subject that was new to me. Up until then I had never seen such a demonstration of pain transcribed directly onto flesh. And as luck would have it, I had hitched myself to the right person. Patty was someone who seemed to hate herself as much as I hated me.

*

The female dining hall had wooden beams running across the high ceilings. Square tables were lined up in rows across the scratched linoleum floor. Arched windows with iron bars ran along one wall. Behind the cafeteria line, a sour-faced patient tossed eggs and dry toast onto people's plates as they passed by. Shuffling behind Patty, I got my food and followed her to a table in the corner. As I sat down and looked around there were both full grown women and young girls. What I noticed was most of them had disgusting table manners. Food dribbling out of open mouths, using their fingers to eat, chewing out loud. It grossed me out.

"These people look fucking crazy," I said.

"Girl, you have no idea." Patty stabbed her fork in the air. "You see that lady over there?"

I followed her gaze to a gaunt woman with droopy brown eyes, and a bottom lip that stuck out.

"She used to be a Hollywood socialite until the syphilis started eating her brain."

"Wait. What?"

"Oh, yeah, girl; syphilis eats the brain. You didn't know that?"

I shook my head in disbelief. I had never heard of such a thing.

Patty pointed her fork again. "And Hannah over there tried to drown her two children in a bathtub."

The woman gazed unblinkingly at her plate, a trembling fork suspended in the air. I felt two things simultaneously at that moment: anger for such a horrendous act and sadness for an unspeakable loss.

"I don't belong here," I said.

"That's what everyone says at first."

But I'm not crazy. These people are different than me."

"I don't belong here either girl, but I actually prefer it here than juvie."

"But why?"

"Once you get privileges, there's more freedom to walk around."

For me, it all boiled down to one thing; I wanted to be home in my own bed, watching my own television and stuffing my face with Oreo cookies. I sat there in silence for the rest of breakfast picking through my food.

*

Once we were back in the dayroom, I felt all the energy evaporate from my body like a gust of wind took it away. I went to go lay down.

I must have fallen asleep because sometime later a staff member was shaking my shoulder. "Wendy, the doctor wants to see you," she said.

"OK. OK, I'm coming," I said, pushing myself up.

I was certain I'd be able to convince Dr. Kramer, the esteemed psychiatrist that I didn't belong there. He'd only have to take one look at me and he'd know. I

slipped on my shoes and made my way down the corridor and knocked on his office door. I heard a muffled
voice from the other side telling me to come in.

When I stepped inside, my breath jackknifed in my
throat when I saw my dad sitting in one of the chairs.
Dad was wearing his public persona of deep concern
underneath sad, hooded eyes. A tightness spread out
across my chest.

He said, "Hi, Wendy. Have a seat," with his usual sarcasm completely hidden.

I looked at the psychiatrist and back at dad. I had no
choice but to sit in the only available chair next to him.
He was heavily doused in Old Spice cologne and I wanted to gag from the smell. Dr. Kramer started speaking
first. "Your Dad is quite concerned about your behavior
lately Wendy, and honestly, so am I."

A pause.

"Why did you want to kill yourself?" he asked.

There was an intense pressure behind my sternum. I
leaned forward ready to use the acting lessons Gretchen
had given me to get out of that wretched place. "I wasn't
really trying to kill myself doctor, I just, I was just was
trying to..." But I struggled to find the right words.

Dad interrupted me. "I'm convinced Wendy is following in her mother's footsteps. In fact, her mother
used to come here all the time until she ended up killing herself when Wendy was seven years old."

It was new to be hearing Dad openly discuss my
mother in front of me. As children, the house was
wall-papered in secrecy. But ever since Irene had told

me the truth about mom's suicide, the bond of silence within our family had been broken. The secret was out.

They talked about me like I wasn't there, and I began to disappear. I was nothing more than a spec of worthless dust that had broken out of orbit with everybody else. At that point it occurred to me that I was in a treacherous no-man's-land where none of the adults could be trusted. Not my Dad. Not the doctor and not the nurses.

When Dr. Kramer, finally asked me again why I did it, I had reached a place of exhaustion. Besides, there was no use trying to convince the enemy that I wasn't crazy because the enemy already had the answers from his books, education and encyclopedias of case studies that sat behind him on his shelf. Suddenly I understood why girls like me and Patty hurt ourselves. We didn't want to commit suicide. Nobody really wants to do that. We were just trying to survive in enemy-occupied territory and we were outnumbered and outgunned. I didn't care anymore. The sadness and failure of the last twenty-four hours was just too much.

"You should tell me why I did it, Doctor Kramer. You're the expert."

The doctor revealed nothing with his poker face, but my little outburst sealed my fate and Dr. Kramer signed the paperwork for a 30-day hold.

*

Two weeks into my hold, I studied the new girl who was sitting in the corner of the dayroom. She had black tearstained cheeks, winged eyeliner and a beehive the size of a fist on the back of her head. I was trying to figure out from a distance whether she was crazy or not. To investigate, Patty and I approached and sat down on both sides of her. After we found out her name was Terry, Patty asked the first question one always asked in there. "Where are you from?"

"San Fernando," Terry replied.

"Cool, girl. That's where I'm from." Patty slapped her a high-five.

Up until then I had no interest in anyone from the Valley. They were into things like cruising Van Nuys Boulevard in a muscle car on a Friday night, while Westsiders like me were into drinking Boones Farm wine on the beach. And while I wouldn't normally hang out with anyone from the Valley, in a mental hospital, I had lowered my standards quite a bit.

"What brings you here?" I asked.

Her pale, green eyes drifted back and forth to each of us. "I'm not crazy, you know. I shouldn't be here."

"You don't have to be crazy to be here," Patty said.

I nodded my head in agreement. I had learned that much by then. In the sixties some kids fell into a gray area and were put in institutions with individuals who were labeled severely "retarded." There wasn't any therapy when I was there. Only Dr. Kramer who was supposed to see you every week, but he often cancelled at the last minute.

"So, what happened?" I asked.

Terry let out a long-exasperated sigh. "My mom was in my face, so I slapped her, and she called the police on me."

Patty shook her head in disgust. "Someone needs to lock up all the parents."

"My mom is a total nut case, that's for sure." Terry's voice was laced with sadness.

I nodded my head, understanding just where she was coming from.

We quickly educated Terry on the do's and don'ts of the mental ward. Explaining how the staff checked on us every night at 3:00 AM, so be sure you're in bed when they sweep their flashlight over your bunk. At breakfast don't eat the chipped beef on toast, better known as shit-on-a-shingle, because we didn't know what they were putting in it. And most importantly, don't take the Thorazine or you'll end up having a thick tongue, drooling, and walking around like a Zombie with droopy eyes. By then I had already mastered a technique of slipping the tan pill in the side of my cheek like a squirrel and spitting out as soon as I was far enough away from the nurse's station. Just then, as if to prove our point, Pam walked in with her short blond hair chopped straight and dangling arms with milk-white skin. There was a stark institutional look about her. Probably because she was one of the kids who had been dropped off by her parents when she was very young. None of us knew the exact details of the story, only that her parents never came to visit her after that.

"Watch this." Patty had a mischievous smile plastered on her face. "Hey, Pam I'm sick."

Pam spun around, her eyes filled with terror. "What? What?" she said.

"I'm sick," Patty repeated.

"No! Not sick. Not sick," Pam said, rushing to one of the nearby pillars which she banged her forehead against.

"What the hell is she doing?" I asked.

"Pam has a meltdown if anyone is sick."

While I knew it was wrong, I couldn't say it because I wanted Patty to continue to be my friend. I needed her in order to survive. I shifted uneasily in my chair as Pam gave her forehead another thump on the pillar. This was just one of the horrible things that I witnessed, but during my stay in the mental hospital I'd see a whole lot more.

*

Day after day it continued. Med lines, meals, school, chores and as many naps as I could squeeze in. Part of the boring routine was the weekly community groups. They were held in a crammed room at the end of the corridor. Only the higher functioning kids were expected to go, while Pam and other "retarded" kids could do whatever they damn well pleased.

A double circle was made with two rows of chairs. This was an hour dedicated to talking about personal problems or going over any business on the unit. Things like: So and so is not doing her chores, the pool table is missing one of its balls, and when are we going to get more books to read? And for me, the most pressing subject was: When can I have my ground privileges?

We were allowed outside in a small inner courtyard, but I had grown tired of looking out at the tops of sycamore trees. Tired of seeing the blue sky and clouds sandwiched between two buildings with slate roofs. Tired of being stuck in a purgatory with a bunch of psycho-cases. The main reason I even did my chores was to get privileges to roam the grounds without a staff member breathing down my neck.

Patty, Terry and I strutted into the group room like we owned the place. "Hey guys, let's sit in the front row today," I said.

"Good idea," Patty agreed.

We were whispering when Flo, an inmate with rows of flesh stomped in wearing an oversized UCLA sweatshirt. I found Flo irritating because she always was kissing ass to staff members. When she sat straight across from me, I gave her the stink eye. She looked away.

Everyone sat up straight when the attending Psych-Tech walked in. Miss Margie was a Mexican woman with thick eye liner and shoulder-length sausage curls. Miss Margie pulled up her sleeve to look at her watch. "Alright girls, it's time to get started." She slapped her hand on the back of her clipboard.

"Good morning, Miss Margie," we all chimed.

"So girls, I want to talk about your chores today. I'm getting complaints from nurses on the other shifts that you're not picking up after yourselves." Miss Margie's narrow eyes scanned the room. Chores could be anything from making your bed, mopping the dayroom, buffing the floor, cleaning the bathroom, setting up chairs and so on. In short, chores were all the things I never did at home because we had a housekeeper.

"You wouldn't leave trash on the floor at home, would you?"

Patty leaned over and whispered, "She obviously hasn't been to my house."

Not wanting to bring any unnecessary attention to myself, I repressed any laughter.

Miss Margie set the clipboard on her lap and used it as a shelf to lean forward on her elbows. "Do you girls have anything else you want to talk about today?" she asked.

I raised my hand. "I do, Miss Margie."

"What's on your mind, Wendy?"

"I've been here a month and I was wondering if I could have my ground privileges?"

At that point I had seen my Dad two times on weekend visits when he took me to the hospital canteen for lunch. Each time I tried to talk him into letting me come home, but he just deferred to the doctor or changed the subject. I was ready to explore the grounds on my own. Miss Margie scrolled through the names on her clipboard with her finger. "Oh, yes. I see you have been here over thirty days." She tilted her head sideways. "Have you had any write-ups?"

"No, ma'am."

"And you've been doing your chores?"

"Yes, ma'am, every day."

She paused, mulling it over in her brain. "Okay, I am going to have to ask the doctor to sign it, but if you are late coming back to the unit, they'll be taken away."

"Thank you so much ma'am." I feigned sincerity while inside my head planning to smoke my first cigarette in a month.

*

The first time I stepped off the unit, I lifted my face towards the sun. I inhaled the smell of wild sage wafting in from the nearby hills. The hospital grounds were a lush green grass. It reminded me of photographs I'd seen of Ireland. Tall 100-year-old sycamore trees lined the streets. A bell tower rose above the adobe tiled roofs.

It was a good thing the three of us had been squirrelling away our meds, otherwise the 80-degree temperature would have caused our pale flesh to turn a lobster red. It happened to other girls who took their Thorazine.

"Let's head over to the canteen," Patty said, skipping out ahead.

The canteen was where inmates could buy personal items like toothpaste, writing paper, postage stamps and stuff like that. You could also sit down at a counter and order a burger and fries. Our plan was to find an inmate who would buy us some cigarettes. They only cost 35 cents back then. A few minutes later we were standing by the payphone scanning the faces of inmates going in and out of the canteen.

"How about that guy?" Terry nodded to a man with wild, black hair and a mustard yellow shirt walking towards us. When we approached him, he stopped in his tracks.

"What do you want?" His fists were clenched.

"Can you buy us a pack of Winstons?" Patty asked, waving the dollar bill, smiling big. "You can keep the change."

He looked us up and down, before taking it. "Wait here," he said, sternly before heading inside.

"Where should we smoke at?" I asked.

"I know the perfect place," Patty said.

A few minutes later the man shuffled out with the goods in his hand and discreetly handed me the cigarettes. It felt like we were making some sort of drug transaction. "Thanks Mister," I said, and we ran off.

Five minutes later we were squatting behind the manicured shrubs in front of the admissions building. I tapped the end of the pack against the back of my hand like my dad would do. He always said it condensed the tobacco making for a smoother smoke. Satisfied, I broke the seal, and tapped out a cigarette.

"Hurry up. We don't have all day." Patty nudged my shoulder.

I struck the match, the red cherry flickered when I inhaled, and the harsh smoke burned the back of my throat. Instantly, my head began to spin. I loved the feeling of dizziness and wanted more. We passed the cigarette until it was gone and Terry crushed the butt under her foot. We were giddy with the illegal nicotine as we popped out from behind the bushes.

"That was cool," Patty said.

"Let's go explore," I said.

Camarillo State Hospital with its Spanish style architecture looked the same as it did when I visited my mom as a little girl. What I didn't know back then was that the sprawling 1500 acres had an auditorium, a bowling alley, and even a thrift store where patients could pick through donated clothes. It was set up to be self-sufficient institution where one could live out the rest of their lives if need be.

But in the late 60's all I was concerned about was smoking or getting high. As we strolled through the hospital, we came to an enticing swimming pool. "Why don't we go swimming?" I asked.

Patty laughed out loud. "Because the patients piss in that pool," she said.

"How do you know?"

"I've seen it. The water turns yellow when they get in." She scowled.

"Ewwww, that's just gross," Terry said.

We kept walking until we came to a place that patients called The Zoo, a high-security unit which had a chain-linked courtyard where severely mentally ill or retarded men were let outside.

"Fucking A. Would you look at that?" Patty shook her head.

"Oh my God." My mouth fell open.

A dozen or more men were inside the fenced enclosure. One of them was rocking back and forth while sitting on a bench. Another was picking up pebbles from the ground. It looked like a multi-car pile-up of broken human beings. While I wanted to turn away, my feet felt glued to the spot. Then I noticed a shirtless man masturbating. There was something overly threatening in the way that man slid his hand up and down his penis while looking at us.

"What the fuck is he doing?" Terry took two steps backwards.

"Oh my God. He's jerking off," Patty said.

Penis in hand, he moved closer and closer to the fence. All three of us screamed and ran in the other direction. When we had gotten far enough away, we slowed down. "That was disgusting." I tried to shake the memory out of my head.

"See what happens when you put human beings in cages?" Patty said. "They start acting like animals."

Eventually we entered the side entrance of one of the off-limits building. The three of us slipped in like thieves, walking down a long, airless corridor. It was creepy, causing the hairs on my neck to stand up.

"I think this is what they call The Hole," Patty said.

"The hole?" I was both curious and scared.

"Where they keep the violent ones."

"But where are the staff?" I asked in a low whisper.

I slowly moved towards one of the doors and peeked into one of the small-chicken-wired windows on my tippy-toes. A woman with a mess of gray hair, was sitting on the edge of her bunk with a blank look on her face. Her gaze of steely-blue eyes landed on me. And in one quick movement, she leaped towards the door causing me to jump back several feet back.

"What happened?" Patty asked.

"There's a crazy woman in there. I think she wants to kill me."

"Let's get out of here," Terry said.

A few minutes later we were crossing the baseball field, I looked at the arched entrance leading out to the open road. I was suddenly struck with a brilliant idea. "We could just walk right off out of here if we wanted to."

"You mean... go AWOL?" Patty said.

I smiled big. "Why not?"

"They'd catch us before we even got off the grounds," Patty said.

"And what would will they do to us then? Lock us up?" I knew a seed had been planted a when Patty and Terry looked at each other. Now all I had to do was wait for it to grow roots.

AWOL

A week later Patty, Terry and I sat at the counter of the canteen-diner, sharing greasy French fries drenched in catsup. A squeaky fan spun overhead. Fly strips hung from the rafters like installations of a strange art nouveau projects. A patient who worked as a waitress with a thick black hairnet filled condiment bottles behind the counter. I thought my life was slipping away as each day passed inside the nut house. My entire body craved an adventure.

"Let's get the fuck out of here." I shoved a fry in my mouth.

"But where will we go?" Terry said.

"We can go to my friend Bobby's house," I said.

Bobby was a guy I knew from the Westside who always seemed to have drugs.

"I'm game," Patty said.

At that point, there was no stopping me. It happened like the flip of a switch. I got up and headed for the cashier. I used the money dad had recently sent me in a Hallmark 'Get Well' card. After paying for the fries, I headed out the door. I walked fast and the girls followed behind. Down Camarillo Street, passing the picnic grounds, my heart pumped with adrenaline.

"This is so crazy," Terry whispered.

I ignored her and once we were at to the exit, I scanned the area for security guards, but there were none. So, the three of us walked under the arch, and just like that, we rushed across the empty country road. As we stepped onto the almond-colored dirt of the farm, it crunched beneath our feet. We all kept turning our heads as to see if anyone was following us, but the coast was clear. My body hummed with excitement as the hospital grounds faded into the distance. The warm air filled my lungs. I hadn't felt so alive in months.

Our grand escape soon turned into more of a physical exertion than I had anticipated with the fields going on and on. With all the starchy food I had been eating I was completely out of breath. Drenched in sweat I wondered why I hadn't called someone to get a ride. My legs felt like I was dragging weights behind me. I was having second thoughts as we trudged through endless rows of produce. We passed a rusty junker car half covered in overgrown weeds. We passed a white cinder-block building. We passed tomatoes and lettuce.

"My feet hurt," Terry scowled.

Patty for some reason started singing a hit song called, Twenty-Five Miles. As adolescents we defined our lives by music. Whether it was the revolutionary songs of Bob Dylan or the funk of Edwin Starr, lyrics bookmarked our big moments. I loved the fact that Patty had picked the perfect song for that moment.

She sang: "Twenty-five miles to go now. My feet are hurting mighty bad, I've been walking for three days and two lonely nights trying to get to my baby somehow." Patty snapped her fingers as her pretty blond head bobbed along with the beat.

I joined her and with the dirt crunching beneath our feet it was like funky background music. A reluctant smile crept over Terry's face as she joined in as well.

"So, we keep on walking... we got to walk on....15 miles to go now, my feet are hurting might bad..."

Singing and laughing we soon forget about our aching feet. Another hour passed and we finally made it to the other side when a white truck appeared on the deserted country road. When I stuck out my thumb, a farmworker with a straw cowboy hat pulled over. We told him we were headed into town and he gestured for us to hop in the back.

We climbed onto the bumper and threw our legs over the side making seats amongst his gardening equipment. We sat down just before the truck took off on its bumpy ride. We got out in Oxnard and extended our thumbs again. It was easy for three girls to get rides and an hour later we were in Los Angeles.

*

It was dusk by the time we stood in the hallway of Bobby's apartment building. A bare bulb hung from the ceiling. The carpet was moldy, the walls smudged with brown streaks. Pushing back the hair from my eyes, I knocked on the door. The peephole went black. When Bobby opened the door, he greeted us with a smile.

Bobby was in his early twenties, with dark, shoulder-length hair, and perfectly arched eyebrows.

"Well, hello girls."

I gave him a tight hug. "I'm so glad to see you Bobby!"

"Come on in."

Walking in I was hit with that musty smell of testosterone and sweat. The place was a landscape of beer bottles and overflowing ashtrays. A black light illuminated posters of dead rock stars. All that bedlam made me feel right at home. I pointed to my companions and said their names by way of introduction. "We just escaped from the mental hospital."

"Oh. Cool. You're fugitives." Bobby nodded approvingly.

"You wouldn't believe how horrible that place is, Bobby," I said.

"How about a little something to help you forget about all that." Bobby pulled out a baggie with red pills from his jacket pocket.

"Oh my God."

"Fucking hell yes!" Patty said.

We were delighted to hear that Bobby had just scored one hundred bootlegged Seconals. We all knew that if you were able to fight the desire to go to sleep on Seconals, there awaited a sensation of delicious drunkenness on the other side. Bobby put two pills in each of our outstretched hands. I threw mine in the back of my mouth and swallowed them dry. Minutes later I felt their pharmaceutical embrace. And then I blacked out.

*

The sound of breaking glass stirred me. The edges of morning crept into the apartment. I could barely lift my head up off the couch. My gaze fell on Patty, who was sleeping on a recliner across the room. Terry was on the floor with a tattered blanket thrown over her.

Apparently, we'd all passed out. I was relieved to see I still had on all my clothes. For a girl, getting wasted could be like turning the lights on in your house while leaving the windows and front door wide open. Anyone could come in. Having unwanted sex or even rape had happened to many girls I knew and up to that point, I had only fooled around with boys. I wasn't looking to have unconscious sex with anyone. But what girl ever is?

"What the hell broke?" I said to no one in particular.

"Oh sorry," Bobby said, coming out of the kitchen. "I dropped something."

"What happened last night?" I reached for a cigarette on the coffee table.

I was searching my memory banks but got nothing but a black hole.

"You don't remember? We stayed up till the wee hours of the night," he said.

The girls were starting to rub the sleep from their eyes.

"Good lord," Patty said. "I still feel loaded."

"You have any coffee Bobby?" I asked.

"I have instant. Help yourself."

I managed to find a saucepan and filled it with water and placed it on the filthy stove. I grabbed the Folger's and put a heaping spoonful into a cup. Bobby came in behind me. "I'm going to a music festival at Big Sur this weekend. Do you girls want to come with?"

"Where's Big Sur?"

"Six hours up the coast. I hear the drive is spectacular."

"Sure. That would be great." Just a day before, the three of us were stuffing soggy hospital fries in our mouths. Anything would be better than that.

Within an hour we were all piling into the back of Bobby's van. Beads hung from the rearview mirror, and the back was packed with camping gear. Bobby reached over my knee and stuffed his little baggie of Seconal into the glove compartment, and we took off.

Unfortunately, I missed the spectacular scenic route because I fell asleep on our way up the coast. I don't remember setting up camp on Friday night. I don't remember eating, but I do remember Bobby doling out some more pills. I remember joining some hippies who were playing guitars and singing songs around a fire when it got dark. I have images of the blurry faces of long-haired boys and beaded girls illuminated by the campfire. Shadows danced on the ground as the flames reached toward the sky.

I used to go camping with my cousins when I was a kid. I even have a yellowed picture, curled at the edges to prove that it actually happened. But just like that faded picture, under the influence of Reds, my experience of Big Sur would also fade.

Come Sunday morning when Bobby delivered the bad news that he was out of Reds, I could hardly believe we had gone through them all. "They're all gone?"

Bobby dangled the empty baggie in the air.

"So, now what?" Patty asked.

"I don't know about you, but I have to go to work tomorrow," Bobby said. "The party's over, ladies, but I can give you a ride back to LA if you want."

While part of me wanted to object, with no more drugs, a feeling of desperation started to creep in. It could have been an after-effect of Seconal. That's when I had a stupid idea.

"Let's go to my house," I said, to the girls. "I'm sure my dad will let us stay there."

"Are you serious?" Patty said.

"Sure." I shrugged.

Riding down Highway 1, I stared at the surf crashing against the shore. Again I was missing the beauty because I was too busy rehearsing excuses inside my head. As crazy as it seemed to go home, there was some part of me that still hoped for my dad and I to have our old relationship back. That he might turn out to be the dad who would be happy to see his daughter at his doorstep.

When we pulled up in front of my house hours later, my stomach was coiled in a knot.

I gave Bobby a big hug. Terry, on the other hand, pressed a kiss against his mouth, which was when I figured out she must have slept with him at some point. You miss a lot of things on Seconals.

A few minutes later, I was knocking on my front door with Patty and Terry standing behind me. When my Dad opened it there was a moment of silence. The creases in his face were deeper than I had ever seen and his hair was grayer. "Wendy, where the hell have you been?"

"Camping," I replied.

"Everyone has been looking for you."

"Can we have something to eat, Dad? We're hungry."

"And whose fault is that?"

Silence.

"Get something in the kitchen."

"Where's Diane at?" I asked, referring to my siblings.

"She works, you know?"

He disappeared to his room.

"Your dad seems pissed off," Patty whispered.

"He's always like that."

We sat at the dining table eating Frosted Flakes when there was a knock on the door. I had a sinking sensation in my gut when I heard the sound of Dad whispering to someone. When I turned around there were two police officers standing with my father.

"Alright girls, the party is over," one officer said, with his handcuffs already out.

"You called the cops?" My eyes narrowed into slits.

"You gave me no choice."

"I hate you so much."

Within minutes we were all cuffed, sitting in the back seat of the squad car on our way back to the mental hospital. As I watched the landscape streak by, I felt like I couldn't take it anymore. Though I never cried, there was an inner weeping that no one could see unless they looked under the façade. I was tired of my Dad, tired of people controlling my life and tired of my family and the secrecy. I wanted to run far, far away and therefore I was already plotting my next escape.

The next morning, I walked into the dayroom ready to formulate another escape plan with my two Road Dogs. I thought maybe we'd head straight up the coast to Big Sur on our own. But when I got to the room, Patty and Terry informed me they were being sent to juvenile hall.

"What? No. You guys can't leave me here." I would have gladly gone to Juvie, if it had meant we could all stay together.

"It's not up to us. We have probation officers, and you don't," Patty said.

I had a vague idea of what a probation officer was but didn't know they could move kids around like pawns on a chess board. "I'm so sorry." I lowered my head. "What am I going to do without you?" It always came back to me. What was I going to do without them? How was I going to go on? How could I go AWOL by myself? In the past parents had labeled me a bad influence on their kids, and somehow that message had seeped deep into my brain. Once again it was all my fault. I felt bad to the core. Gravely corrupted, so it's better that you stay away from me.

I had fallen asleep when the girls left. I couldn't bear saying good-bye to them. I didn't understand it yet, but any time someone left me it seemed directly linked to other losses in my life. If I had actually seen them walk out the door, other grief like my mother's death could have come dislodged and I couldn't risk that. It might suffocate me.

For the next few weeks, I refused to get close to anyone. It came at too great a cost. Instead, I stared blankly at cartoons or anything else playing on the tv during the day. During the nights the ward crawled with noises. Inmates got up and walked the hallways. The staff's flashlights would sweep over me as they checked beds.

Even though we were told that the hospital was a place to get some much needed "rest," it was hard to sleep in there.

Two weeks later Dad came to take me out on a pass. As we sat at House of Pancakes, we didn't talk about his calling the police or me running away. It could have been a perfect moment to explore the rift that had developed between us. To tell him I was sorry for being such a pain in the ass. But instead, we sat there pretending like none of it ever happened.

"Diane got a job in the cafeteria at St. John's hospital," Dad said.

"Good for her." A twinge of jealousy ran up my spine. My sister was always more responsible than me. Getting good grades in school, staying out of trouble, and now she had a job. "Can you pass the syrup, please?"

Dad passed me the sticky bottle of Aunt Jemima. The same mass-produced syrup they used in the hospital, but it tasted better outside the walls.

"Maybe you could get a babysitting job when you get out?"

"Who's going to leave their kids with me?"

"You'd be surprised."

I had been reading cues from my Dad ever since I was a kid. I could tell he was in one of those warmer, guilt-laced moods that I could take advantage of. "Does that mean I can come home?"

Dad tapped out one of his Camels from the pack, stuck it in between his lips and struck a match. He was stalling, something he always seemed to enjoy. I was getting annoyed but tried not to show it.

"You think you're ready to stay out of trouble?"

"Dad. I promise I'll stay out of trouble. I just want to come back home." I teared up.

I meant every word of it too. More than anything I wanted to be normal. I wanted to be like those girls who went to Friday night football games who cheered for the team. Things like school pride that had always eluded me. I wanted to be more like kids who finished their homework. But they must have gotten the rules to the game called life that I wasn't privy to.

"Let me talk to the doctor," he said, gray smoke swirling above his head.

I let out a long sigh. It was a good sign. And while it was the doctor who had to sign the papers, it would take Dad's blessing in order for him to sign my release form. But I also knew that Dad's mind could be swayed given the point of view of someone in a position of authority. I would remain cautiously optimistic just the same.

*

Three months after I first arrived, I was told by one of the psych-techs to report to Dr. Kramer's office. I took a deep breath and knocked on the open door.

"Have a seat," he said, barely looking up.

His desk made it feel like an entire island was between us. I sat in the chair chewing on my cuticle in silence as he read my chart. A chart that wasn't as big as some of the other patients, but way too big for me. It had all the notes from the nurses from all the shifts. They were required to document our behavior every day. My chart also had the test I had filled out that asked questions like: Do you believe in God? Do you hate your parents? Do you ever have thoughts of hurting others? I had tried to answer it the way a normal person might, but the questionnaire tried to trick you with the same question framed in a different way. Was that to see if you were lying? Or were they giving you opportunity to redeem yourself? I had no idea.

Finally, Dr. Kramer looked up and glanced over his bifocals. "So, Wendy, how's everything going with you?"

"I've been staying out of trouble."

"Yes. I've been told."

"So, can I go home now?"

"That's what I want to talk to you about." He picked up a cup from his desk and took a sip of coffee. "I'm a bit concerned about your relationship with your father. Do you think you've addressed your resentments towards him?"

"Yes, I have, doctor. He's been taking me out on passes every week. He orders the chocolate chip pancakes, but I prefer the strawberry with loads of whipped cream."

"Are you still as angry at him?"

Act normal. Act normal.

"I've come to accept a lot of things in my life."

"And what about your mother?"

Of course, he wanted to talk about my mother. Everyone did, except for me. "I'm okay with that too."

He gave me a weak smile. "You've made a lot of progress while you've been here. I am going to authorize your release."

"Really?" I beamed him one my most brilliant smiles, all teeth and innocence. "Doctor Kramer, I just want to thank you for everything. You've really helped me a lot," I said, lying through those same teeth.

"I'm glad I could help in some small way."

"Yes sir, you have."

*

The next day, my few belongings sat in the back seat as we drove down Pacific Coast Highway. Dad's salt and pepper hair was held in place with Butch wax. He held out his pack and offered me one of his Winstons. Dad always liked to change his cigarette brands for some reason. I took it, recognizing it as the peace offering as it was, and pushed in the lighter. A minute later the red-hot coil popped out of the dashboard. I lit my cigarette. It was quiet as I gazed at the moving landscape, evidence we were getting farther away from the hospital. Once we hit Malibu there were a few lone surfers cutting through the blue-gray waves, the stone-gray sky above them. A cool wind found its way through a narrow slice of open window, whipping my hair into a frenzy.

"You'll need to check in with the admissions office at school on Monday," he said.

"Where do they think I've been?"

"I had to tell them the truth."

"Oh great. Nothing like everybody knowing my business."

After growing up with Dad telling us not to talk about my mother's mental illness, I feared someone knowing my flaws they could somehow be used against me later, so I was skilled in secret keeping.

"Not everyone knows," he said. "Just the administration office so you wouldn't fail this semester."

Shame slithered up my spine. I would not only have to face the humiliation of people knowing I was in the nuthouse, I would probably have to catch up on a shit-load of school credits. Camarillo didn't offer a comprehensive curriculum. Just a workbook that allowed you to move at your own pace, and my pace had been extremely slow.

An hour later we were driving down our palm-tree lined street.

Dad turned off the ignition. "Look Wendy, I'm really excited you're home. Let's make this work this time." He leaned over and gave me a kiss on the cheek. His words felt more like a warning and he sealed it with a kiss. I bit my lip and tilted my head the other way.

When I walked in the front door everything was quiet, empty and cold. There wasn't a soothing feeling of being home. Home was nothing more than a place to sleep and eat.

Our housekeeper Irene came in with her dyed red-orange hair looking like she had just come from the hairdresser. "Welcome home Wendy." Irene wrapped her thick arms around me for a hug. I could already smell alcohol seeping from her pores. I squirmed from her embrace.

"I need to put my stuff away," I said, excusing myself.

"Of course, darling," she said. Dad was already making himself a drink at his well-stocked bar.

My shared bedroom with Diane had two twin beds with matching white dressers. A poster of Bob Dylan's Blond on Blond album was taped to the wall. There was a small RCA television in the corner perched on a stand. I stepped toward the mirror that hung on the closet door. It had been two months since I examined myself in a full-length mirror. My wispy tangled brown hair looked a mess. My face was speckled with blemishes. My body was thick from too much starchy hospital food. My tummy rolled over the waistband of my jeans. I couldn't stand the image staring back at me. I flung myself onto the bed. The mattress rose up on all sides as if to swallow me.

I didn't know it back then, but my family could easily trigger me. The people in my house who were living within a construct of imposed silence connected me to a deeper grief. My brothers, my sister, my father were all part of a collective pain. Just being around them caused me to feel a profound aloneness and I didn't quite understand what was going on.

And then. Like a revelation: I wanted to get high.

Not with Thorazine, either. That didn't count.

I wanted to shack up with a dealer who could keep me loaded all the time.

I wanted to be obliterated.

I didn't care what happened to my body.

I just didn't want to feel anything.
I wanted to disappear.

Runaway

Two months after I got home from Camarillo, Tara and I were sitting on the bleachers together. Tara had the body of a runway model with thick blond hair that cascaded down her shoulders to the middle of her back. We had become friends after I got kicked out of St. Monica's.

I was etching my initials into the soft, splintery wooden bench with a paperclip. I knew better than to leave my entire name amongst the other initials and proclamations of love or it could be used against me later on.

"Look at those stupid girls," Tara said, glaring off into the distance.

"Which ones?" I followed her gaze.

"All of them. Those snobby bitches make me want to puke."

She was referring to the loud, happy teenagers sitting on the grass eating their lunches. Some had their hair piled up in beehives, held together by copious amounts of hairspray, while others had short bobs that flipped at the ends. I didn't think any of the girls were intentionally trying to arouse our envy, but that's exactly what they did.

"Fucking clueless bitches," I said.

I was trying my best to stay out of trouble when Tara made this announcement: "I'm going to run away."

"Really? Why?"

"I hate my stepdad." I knew Tara's mother had recently remarried and the new hubby was strict.

"That bad, huh?"

"He's trying to tell me what I can, and can't do, and he's not even my dad."

Silence. Then I said, "I'll go with you if you run away."

"Really? You would do that?"

I wanted to show her what real friendship looked like, but I also wanted to get away from the constant drama and craziness going on at home. "Of course," I said, like it was a no brainer.

"Where would we go?"

Staring off in the distance I spotted a girl with two long braids, dressed in a bright orange tie-dyed, t-shirt. "We can see where the open road takes us."

*

Early the next morning Tara and I met by the flagpole in front of school. I was dressed in bell-bottom jeans and a sweatshirt. I'd also brought a backpack stuffed with a toothbrush, a change of clothing and a dozen Twinkies, in case we got hungry. Tara was wearing a cool brown rawhide jacket with fringe that hung from the back of her arms like wings.

"You sure you want to do this?" Tara's forehead was crinkled up.

"Totally."

That was it. An hour later we were standing on the Pacific Coast Highway with our thumbs out. It took less than five minutes before a green and white Volkswagen van with flowers and a peace sign pulled over. Tara climbed in the back and I got in the front. Instantly I was hit with the smell of stale cigarette smoke and Patchouli oil. Strands of beads hung from the rear-view mirror. The driver was a guy with long brown hair, a straggly beard, and a rawhide vest worn over a linen shirt.

"Where you girls headed?" he asked.

"That way." I pointed in front of me.

"Well, what a coincidence. I'm going that way too," he smiled.

"Groovy."

"My name is Jeff by the way."

We told him our names.

"We just ran away from home," Tara blurted out.

Jeff tilted his head sideways. "Oh really? Runaways?"

"Our parents suck," I said, as if no other explanation was needed.

"I dig it man. I left home when I was seventeen."

"Wow. That's really cool," Tara said.

As we drove up the coast, I watched the waves reaching up like fingers on the shore. I loved everything about the ocean. The mere sight of it could put me at ease. When we came to a red-light Jeff hit the brakes causing empty bottles and beer cans to roll forward from underneath the seat.

"Looks like you had a party," I said.

"Oh yeah, sorry about that."

"No problem."

The salty wind was whipping my hair in my face.

"What do you do, Jeff?" Tara said, leaning forward.

"I'm a singer-songwriter."

I liked the sound of that. He seemed like a free spirit.

"Right now, I happen to be living in the caves."

"What caves?" Tara asked.

"In the canyon."

"I've never met a cave man before," I smiled.

"You chicks are welcome to come check it out."

Looking around Tara gave an enthusiastic nod.

"Yeah. Okay," I said.

A few minutes later the bottles and cans crashed again as we made a sharp right turn. Topanga Canyon Boulevard was a narrow, windy road, curling through the burnt orange Santa Monica Mountains. As we drove deeper into the canyon, I stuck my head out the window, causing my hair to windmill in my face. The chaparral-covered hills with steep rock out-cropping's were breathtaking. I gazed down at the creek that rushed over massive boulders and rocks below. The raw beauty and energy of it all caused my blood pressure to drop a good ten points.

Pulling my head in, I asked Jeff. "Are we still in L.A?"

"Yup."

"I never even knew this place existed."

"Topanga is a well-kept secret," Jeff smiled.

"Well, I've had plenty of practice keeping secrets in my life," I said.

"Haven't we all," Jeff said, in a matter of fact tone.

The van pulled onto a sliver of dirt by the side of the road. "Here we go, ladies." Jeff reached over and picked up his bag.

Tara and I grabbed our backpacks and crawled out of the van.

"So, where are the caves?" I asked.

Jeff pointed. "Down there."

"Looks sort of dangerous." Tara's face was all scrunched up.

"I climb it every day." Jeff swung his long leg over the guardrail.

Tara and I followed, dropping down onto a narrow clearing that was being strangled off by a thick layer of prickly underbrush and plants. Beyond the ledge was a dramatic drop into what seemed like a dark abyss.

"Oh shit," I said.

"I know. I know," Tara said.

"If you start to lose your balance grab onto something," Jeff said.

"Have you ever fallen before?" I cupped my hands over my mouth.

"Just once...." he said, without stopping.

As we made our way down, the loose dirt started to slip beneath us.

"Watch out for poison ivy," Jeff yelled.

"What's it looks like?"

"Red and orange with almond shaped leaves."

All of a sudden, I lost my balance and fell. I grabbed a handful of shrubbery to keep myself from going further down the hill. I pushed myself up and dusted the dirt off my butt. We see-sawed down the embankment. In some places it was so steep I had to sit down and scoot along on my butt.

Out of breath, we finally made it to the bottom. I noticed how everything was super quiet except for the water gushing in the nearby creek. The smell of sage and pine hung in the air. "Wow. It's so quiet here," I said to no one in particular.

"This way, girls." Jeff wanted us to keep moving.

Dry leaves and twigs crunched beneath our feet. I turned to Tara and said, "How the hell are we going to get back up?"

"Can't go up when it's dark, that's for sure," she said.

As we followed the creek downstream, Jeff abruptly stopped in front of a huge gray boulder. "Camp is on the other side of this," he said, patting the rock with his hand. My neck craned as I gazed upward. The boulder was the size of a small house.

"But how do we get over?" Tara asked.

"Just watch me and do the same thing." Jeff started to climb with a surprising agility for a man who had to be over thirty. He used the tips of his fingers and toes to shimmy up the side. He made it look so easy, and seconds later he was at the top, cupping his hands over his mouth, he yelled, "Okay, girls, come on up. One at a time."

Tara went first. I bit my lip as she snaked her way up the side. I was afraid she would fall and break a bone. Then what? But Tara didn't fall and when she made it to the top, I let out a long sigh of relief.

"It's not as hard as it looks," Tara said, cheering me on.

My heart was pounding as I inserted the tips of my fingers into the same dusty crevices that they had both used. I felt the hard, unrelenting rock beneath the front of my body. The toes of my sneakers found a small ledge as I reached my right arm overhead, searching for the next crack. When I found something to hold onto, my thigh and calf muscles tightened as I pushed myself up a few more feet. Reaching with my left arm to a crevice, I pulled myself up again. Twenty pounds over my ideal weight, and a half-pack-a day-smoker, I quickly became out of breath. When I made it the top, I felt a great sense of satisfaction.

Standing next to Tara and Jeff, I gazed down at a waterfall with dark water gushing out from between two rocks. I was surprised to see a bunch of naked hippies standing waist high in a swimming hole with a crescent slice of sand encircling a private beach. It was the first time I had seen so much exposed flesh in one place. Embarrassment rippled up my spine. I had to look away.

A guy with his dick dangling between his thighs yelled, "Who are your friends, Jeff?"

"They're runaways," he said.

"Well, come on in girls," Dick man said. "The water is refreshing."

"Ah... No. I'm good, but thanks," I replied, holding up my hand.

We kept descending the boulder but getting down was much easier than going up. Toward the bottom, I pushed off and landed with a thud on the crunchy gravel. I noticed the shallow caves Jeff was talking about at the base of the jagged mountain. Each opening was stuffed with a sleeping bag and scattered articles of clothing. I could see why all the hippies would want to stay there. It was the ideal place to live off the grid.

A big-breasted girl with hair like chocolate fondue was stirring a pot over an open fire as smoke drifted toward the sky.

"Do you girls want some of my special brewed cowboy coffee?" she asked.

"Sure." I shrugged.

Tara and I sat on a log in front of the fire.

"How did you guys meet Jeff?" she asked.

"We were thumbing it on PCH."

"Groovy." She stirred the simmering liquid in the pot. "They call me Sunshine around here."

"Do you have parents, Sunshine?" Tara asked. "I mean, how do you live down here?"

"My parents were always up my ass, so I ran away."

"Yeah, my parents were up my ass too," Tara said, nodding.

A few minutes later, Dick man came and sat on a rock, his flaccid penis nearly touching the ground. I averted my eyes as Tara dug her elbow deep into my ribs.

"Hello ladies." He smiled.

Making sure to avoid looking at the penis, I gazed just over his head.

"Welcome to our casa," he said, smiling directly at Tara.

Minutes later Sunshine pulled out a fat joint. It was getting late and the sky had an orange, pinkish glow. By then all the other hippies were joining us. When the pot came around to me, I took a hit. The smoke was harsh and burned the back of my throat. Coughing, I passed it on to Tara.

As we got buzzed, we listened to stories backed by the sound of water falling over rocks a few feet away. Smiles emerged in the blurry orange light from the flames. A half-gallon of Red Mountain wine got passed around and everyone took swigs directly from the bottle.

I had a good buzz going on when one of the younger guys started playing his guitar and singing, Heart of Gold, by Neil Young. My shoulders swayed to the sound. The sweetness of his voice coaxed everyone else to join in. We all knew the song and it sounded like a chorus bouncing off the canyon walls and reverberating into the ethers.

I want to live.

I want to give.

I've been a miner for a heart of gold. ...

The words never felt truer to me than they did in that moment.

We stayed up until the fire started going out. Some of the people said goodnight before drifting off into the blackness. I watched in horror when Dick Man took Tara by the hand and guided her to his cave.

Suddenly, I was struck with fear. Where am I going to sleep?

As if reading my mind, Jeff said, "You're welcome to share my sleeping bag."

I put my palms closer to the fire and took a deep breath. "Okay. Cool," was all I managed to say.

Jeff stood up and I watched him walk away.

A jittery feeling took over my entire body.

I was trapped. While I had let plenty of guys feel me up or put their fingers inside me, I hadn't actually gone all the way with anyone yet. I was afraid Jeff might want to have sex. After all, weren't the hippies all about free love?

A few minutes later I found myself fully clothed worming my way into Jeff's sleeping bag. Although I might have had sex with him had he tried, Jeff only went as far as holding me in his arms. What I remember mostly was how the moon shone like a bleached oyster shell and the zillion silvery stars, flashing like sequins on a black velvet cocktail dress in the sky.

"Gorgeous, right?" Jeff asked.

"It's, it's so beautiful."

Jeff may not have noticed, but tears had welled up in my eyes. With a mind like a finely-tuned torture-device, it was rare for me to notice such beauty. As I drifted off to sleep, I wondered if my Dad was looking for me, but eventually my entire body merged with the blackness of the night.

*

The next morning my mouth tasted like sour milk. The ground was hard. I gazed up past the jagged, rusty-colored cliffs. I imagined Dad would be on his second cup of coffee by now. Or perhaps he was on hold with the authorities filing a missing person's report. What happened to my intention to avoid getting into trouble? Why couldn't I stop doing the very things I didn't want to do? Sometimes it felt like Mom had planted dark parts of herself inside me, and I was left with the task of figuring out what was her, and what was me.

Behind me, Jeff let out a long sigh. I turned and looked at the strange man. While I was relieved he hadn't tried anything during the night, I also wondered why. Was I not cute enough? I looked down at my own body, my hands, my legs, my soft belly. I decided I was too fat, ugly. Before I was even upright, my torture-device of a brain started in.

I heard the hushed tones of girls' voices coming from the nearby fire. I got up and put on my tennis shoes. The gravel crunched beneath my feet. I sat down on the log next to Tara, and like a big sister, she draped a blanket over my shoulder, tucking me into a cocoon.

"Coffee?" Sunshine asked, holding out a chipped cup.

"Yes, please."

The first sip left coffee grounds on my tongue. I spat them unto the dirt. Sunshine poked around the fire with a stick causing orange sparks to release towards the sky. Flames crackled and licked at the blackened branches. The sound of the creek trickling over smooth rocks behind us gave me a momentarily sense of calm. Out here, time didn't answer to the bell of first period or a curfew set by Dad. The pulse of the earth rose up through the ground and into my feet. The birds spoke to each other across treetops, calling and responding. I had the rare experience of being aligned to the moment, a feeling of peace, until Tara brought me back to reality.

"Do you think your dad called the cops?"

"My dad calls the police whenever we talk back to him. So, yeah. I'm sure he did."

"Right." She nodded.

Just then Dick Man appeared. Mercifully, he was dressed in sweatpants and a t-shirt and his junk was not on display. Without a word, he reached both his arms toward the sky, pressed his hands together, before falling over and touching the ground. Then he pulled himself up and did the same thing over again. This time he released a long, exaggerated sigh. I couldn't help watching him. In some ways he reminded me of Jesus Christ. After several of these, he released an OM, the sound swelling to a crescendo before he bowed his head with his hands at his chest in prayer. Finally, he sat down on a boulder across from us. "Top of the morning to you, ladies," he said.

When Tara smiled, I could tell by the dreamy look on her face that they'd hooked up the night before. He smiled back at her with a hunger in his eyes. Feeling awkward, I filled the silence with chatter. "What do you guys do around here all day?"

His head slowly turned toward me, his eyes looking somewhere in the distance. "You know, man. We chill out, play music, swim, go to the store for supplies, and sometimes we even trip out on acid."

That all seemed a little too mellow for my tastes. I wanted adventure. I wanted to meet people. I wanted to get high on something other than acid.

As more people woke up, they gathered around the fire, and Sunshine, with a molasses smile on her lips, extended cups of coffee to all of them. Soon there was a cluster of hippies, chatting it up. The girls were draped in dresses and looked dirty from head-to-toe. The men wore beards and long hair. Strands of beads adorned the whole barefoot lot. In theory, I liked this hippie community, but I didn't quite... belong. But then again, I never felt like I belonged. Anywhere.

I nudged Tara in the ribs and gave my head a little nod. She knew I wanted to talk so we excused ourselves saying we both had to pee. We disappeared behind a huge rock and made a plan to hitchhike. Hitchhiking always bore promise: we'd see where the open road took us, who it delivered. After all, we didn't have to go to school, so we were determined to play.

Once back at the fire Tara turned to Dick Man. "We're thinking of going out today," Tara said. "Do you mind if we come back later on?"

"Mi casa es su casa." He opened up his arms as if he held the entire world inside his chest.

*

An hour later, Tara and I stood on the road and stabbed our thumbs into the air. I was dusty from climbing up the side of the hill. The dirt from the canyon felt like a second skin.

"So, did you...?" I asked.

"Yeah." She looked away.

The more sex my friends were having, the more my virginity stood out, like a glowing neon sign that said, 'unfuckable' across my chest. "Well? How was it?"

"He seemed to like it."

"How could you tell?"

"He made a lot of weird noises. You know, like an animal."

None of us really knew anything about sex. It was this mysterious vacuum, churning our interest and appetites. Intercourse was never discussed in school or by most parents, so you were left to comb through your friends' experiences, trying to file away the things that might be useful to you.

"Well, did you like it?"

"It kind of hurt." A sadness passed over her cat eyes. I didn't understand what that look was about, but I would learn later on when I too would join the elite ranks of women having empty sex with blurry men.

"Anything happen with you and Jeff?"

"We just kind of hugged is all."

She was about to ask something else when a Chevy pulled up. We both jumped inside and found an old man with a shock of gray hair behind the wheel. "Where you girls headed?" He smiled through yellow teeth.

"Venice Beach."

Thus began our adventures of being cave dwellers by night and hitchhikers by day.

*

Venice Beach was a place that attracted rebellious types. When we got there the boardwalk was teeming with bikini-clad girls looping gracefully on roller skates, hippies beating Congo drums, and thick-muscled men pumping weights. It was easy for a runaway to disappear in a psychedelic, sub-culture with these types of characters.

We stopped in front of the shuttered POP, a theme park that had once offered my family wholesome fun. The entrance was boarded up now with graffiti painted plywood. Beyond that I could see a partial outline of the hazardous roller coaster obscured by cracked walls. Nothing in there but sea-breeze and silence.

When my father used to take us there, I would lose myself on the rides. Faint music, laughter, and happy screams filled those hot summer days. A rollercoaster, a big wheel, a house of mirrors. One of my favorite rides was The Graviton, where you would stand with your back to the wall in a cylinder and the floor would drop out from underneath your feet while it spun and spun. I had to make sure I didn't eat beforehand, or I'd end up throwing up.

There was no more laughter, no screams of delight, and no smell of cotton candy or popcorn in the air. Weeds rose up through cracks in the asphalt, seagulls circled above our heads. Standing in front of the rotted theme park, ash from the campfire on my skin, I was the one who felt like a ghost.

As Tara and I continued to stroll down the boardwalk, my eyes landed on a coffin-sized pay phone. An insistent need came over me. "I want to call home."

"You're kidding, right?"

"I need to let my dad know I'm alright."

"But what if they trace the call?"

"It's not like I'm a murderer or something."

Tara raised her eyebrows and shrugged

I went to the nearby phone booth and the door collapsed behind me as Tara waited outside. I put in a dime and punched in the numbers. After a few rings Irene picked up. "Can I talk to my dad?"

"Wendy, where are you?" Irene sounded out of breath. "Your dad's worried sick."

"Can I talk to him please?"

"He's not here."

I lowered my head. "Please tell him I'm okay."

"Your father is worried...."

I slammed the receiver down and let out an exasperated sigh. I hadn't been gone 24 hours and I already wanted to go home. I don't know why I called my Dad. Or, maybe I do know. I was confused. Tired. And as rocky as our relationship had become, there were still echoes of a more innocent time– a time when he had cherished me. And I, him. I longed to feel safe, like when I was a little girl curled up in his lap. And some small part of me thought that safety should come from him.

The Raid

After two weeks of cave life I had a nasty rash that was having its way with me. Blotchy, raised pink skin with tiny bumps appearing on the back of my legs and in between my fingers. It itched like crazy, and no amount of will power, which was nonexistent anyway, could keep me from scratching it. I suspected it was a bad case of poison oak, but I was used to ignoring my health needs unless I was made to go to the doctor.

As uncomfortable as it was, it didn't prevent us from hitchhiking every day. Tara and I went back and forth to Venice, roughly 13 miles one way, so many times it was almost like we were on a treasure hunt. The goal was simple: meet people who were holding drugs and see if we could get some.

One day after climbing up the side of the hill, Tara and I stuck out our thumbs. Within minutes two stoners in a battered station wagon pulled over to pick us up. A blond guy sitting shotgun, hooked a forearm over the car door and leaned out the window. "Where you girls headed?" he asked.

"Where you headed?" Tara replied, with a hand on her hip.

"San Fernando Valley."

"Us too." She smiled.

"Well, hop on in then."

We climbed in, plopping down on the back seat that had stuffing coming out of its cracks. We exchanged introductions while assessing their character. The driver, Sal, had a long angular face with wavy jet-black hair and a NY Yankees baseball cap. The blond guy was David. He turned the rock music down from a tinny radio in the dashboard and turned sideways to talk to us. They seemed safe enough.

"Where you guys from?"

"Santa Monica," Tara said.

Sal turned his head sideways, keeping one eye peeled on the road. "Shouldn't you be in school?"

"We ran away from home. We live in the caves now," Tara said.

"What's that like?" David said, raising an eyebrow.

"It's actually pretty cool," I said.

"Do you two girls like to get high?" Sal asked.

"Well that depends on what you're talking about?" I said.

They gave each other a look. "Have you ever tried coke?" Sal asked.

We both wanted to seem cool, adult, obviously hip beyond our years. But the fact was neither of us had, so we confessed our lack of experience.

"Would you like to try some?"

This time, Tara and I looked at each other. I could tell by the sparkle in her eye she was game.

"Yes," we responded in unison.

"We have some at our apartment in North Hollywood."

"We got nothing else to do," I said.

Forty minutes later, we were in the dimly lit hallway of their apartment building. David opened the door of their unit. I was hit immediately with the smell of stale cigarettes smoke. After two weeks of living in nature under the stars the unventilated air made my throat close up. A ceiling fan swayed back and forth as it turned in the living room. There were empty beer and wine bottles everywhere. The thick blue curtains were closed to block out any light.

"Sorry. We had a little party last night." David tossed an empty pizza box from the couch. Tara and I sat down next to each other, my arm touching hers. Somehow, the contact made me feel like nothing could happen to us together.

"Make yourself comfortable," he said. "We'll be right back."

They disappeared down the hall.

Tara turned and whispered, "You think these guys are safe?"

"I'm not getting any weird vibes. Are you?"

Vibes were how we determined the perv factor when we hitchhiked. So far, it had served us well. Tara shook her head, "no."

A few minutes later David came back holding a round mirror with four powdery white lines the size of toothpicks running across the top. Excitement and fear swelled inside me. In that moment I just wanted to experience something new, illegal and slightly taboo. My chemistry reacted before I did, lighting up all my nerve endings.

"Who wants to go first?" David said, holding a rolled-up $1-dollar bill.

"You go," I said.

I watched as David shoved the end of the $1-dollar bill into his nostril while closing his other nostril with the tip of his index finger. He leaned over and sucked one of the lines up like a human vacuum cleaner. His whole body jerked back as he shook his head causing his blond hair to whip him in the face.

"This shit is fucking good."

Tara nudged my arm. "You go first," she said.

My stomach was churning as I took the tight cylinder in between my index finger and thumb. I leaned over and with one sweep, inhaled one of the lines off the mirror. Instantly, my sinuses were set on fire. A soothing warmth filled my lungs and brain. The blood rushed to my head. My face was flushed. Every cell in my body vibrated. My vision sharpened, the edges of things became more precise, more incredible. A euphoria rushed through me. This was a high I had never felt before. I felt invincible. This was where I wanted to be all the time.

"Do you like it?" Tara asked.

"Its soooo fucking good."

I handed her the dollar bill. With that, Tara leaned over and sucked up the next toothpick line of coke. When she was done, she fell backward onto the couch saying, "Oh my god, Oh my god. Oh my god."

Although we might not have realized it at the time, both of us had just graduated. While there would always be alcohol, pills and party drugs in our future, our taste for the more refined, more expensive powder would stay imprinted on our psyche from that night forward.

I don't remember how much coke we did, but I remember the urgency of it all. We stumbled over each other's words, trying to share our brilliant ideas with each other. Cosmic realms were reaching down to channel inspiration that the world had never known before. I was feeling completely at home with these guys. They were like old friends who we had known for years.

Sal got quiet and his penetrating eyes trained on Tara. She lowered her head and smiled self-consciously. Sal leaned in and kissed her on her mouth. There was often an expectation if guys turned you on with free drugs, you'd have to repay them the favor. With cocaine, I was glad to oblige if it just meant making out.

David was staring at me and ready to make his move. Every cell of my body screamed to be touched. I was ready. I leaned forward.

Then, a loud knock on the front door. We all froze. I looked over at Sal, who'd pulled away from Tara's mouth. David leaped up and grabbed the mirror wiping it on the back of his leg. I knew we were in trouble.

Another knock, followed by the sickening sound of wood breaking as the front door right next to us came crashing in. A dozen officers rushed us in a wave of blue.

"HANDS IN THE AIR!," a sergeant yelled with his gun pointed at us.

Holy fucking shit!

My hands were shaking as I put them up. My breath jack-knifed in my throat. The high from moments before seemed to evaporate. A young officer with a buzzed cut quickly assessed the situation. "You girls come with me."

Tara and I were escorted into the kitchen. He told us to sit down. "Put your hands on the table," he ordered.

The Formica table had a bag of half eaten French fries and burger wrappers on top. I pushed them aside and placed my palms face down and Tara did the same. The sound of loud voices and banging came from the room we had just left.

The young rookie put his gun back in his holster, and leaned back, resting against the kitchen counter and crossing his thick arms over his chest.

"How old are you girls?" he asked.

"Fourteen."

"How do you know these two characters?"

"We met them today hitchhiking." In a display of how young we really were, Tara started to cry.

"So, you came home with them?"

"They wanted to hang out."

"And that sounded fun?" He snorted, shaking his head. "Did you ever think they might rape you?"

"They seemed like nice guys," I said, in my defense.

"They're drug dealers."

"Oh my god. Really? We didn't know. I swear."

"They supply most of the Valley."

Just our luck to get a ride with the most wanted drug dealers in the Valley.

"Are you girls runaways?"

"Yes. We are..." With a sudden surge of shame, I lowered my head.

"Are you high right now?"

"No. No." Both of us were very emphatic in our assertions of how high we were most definitely not.

His green eyes were calm. Friendly even. I didn't want to lie to him.

"Well, maybe we did just a little bit of coke." I held up my finger and thumb to show him the insignificant amount that I was referring to. The cop gave us a stern lecture on the dangers of doing hard core drugs as he tried to scare us with things that could happen to foolish young girls. I'm sure it was all very pertinent information. None of which registered because I liked the feeling I had gotten earlier too much to be deterred by some well-intentioned cop. But pretending we were on the same page, Tara and I nodded our pretty little heads and gazed at him with concern in our eyes.

A few minutes later we were led through the living room where the curtains were now open. The room was trashed with bottles and cigarette butts strewn all over the floor after the cop's had done a thorough search. Sal was sitting on the couch with his face full of terror and his hands cuffed behind him. David wasn't anywhere around, so I figured they had taken him to the bedroom. Although I had no interest in police procedures, I was getting a lesson on how cops separate criminals when they interrogate them.

We were driven to Van Nuys police station in a squad car where our parents were called.

A few hours later my Dad arrived, his brow furrowed and his jaw pulled tight. "You know how worried I've been?" he said, looking down at me as I sat cuffed to a bench.

"I'm sorry Dad..." I lowered my head.

The arresting officer uncuffed me and gave Dad a date when I was to appear in juvenile court. I was then released into his custody. As we walked to the nearby parking structure, Dad was limping, favoring his good leg. But once inside the car, he slapped me just as hard as he could across the face. "What is wrong with you anyway?" he yelled, spit flying from his mouth.

I didn't have an answer for him or for myself. I had no idea what was wrong with me. I just felt broken inside.

The slap took my breath away, but I hardened my insides and willed myself not to cry. As we drove home in silence, I chanted a thousand fuck yous inside my head. Right then, I hated my dad and couldn't wait till I could run away again.

*

It had been two weeks since I was arrested. Dad was still pissed off, so I stayed in my room trying to avoid the palpable tension bouncing off the walls. My brothers and sister barely talked civilly anymore, and seeing how I was the most recent embarrassment, that went double for me. Our family always seemed to be trying to cover up some scandalous thing one of us had done. It used to be my mother's mental illness, now it could be any one of us, who were acting out. Even Diane was drinking a lot with her friends.

While a big part of me wanted to be back at the caves I still had some of that nasty rash from poison oak all over my body from going down the mountain.

Even Calamine lotion didn't stop the ceaseless itching. Through my objections, Dad had made an appointment for me with Dr. Simon, our long-standing, family physician.

In the waiting room, Dad sat on one side of me and a small boy sat on the other his legs kicking in the air. Every time the nurse opened the door to call someone in, his eyes went wide, and his legs stopped kicking and dangled several inches from the floor. I assumed he felt the same dread about seeing the doctor I felt. I figured all kids did.

Eventually, a young nurse, not a single hair out of place, escorted me with her wedged white shoes squeaking down the hall. In the exam room, she gave me a paper-thin robe to put on. A few minutes later I was sitting on the edge of the exam table when my Dad came in. "Why are you in here?" I asked.

"I need to talk to the doctor."

"It's just a rash. I can tell him myself."

Silence. When the door opened again, Dr. Simon, with a shock of white hair marched in with the prongs of his stethoscope jutting from his white coat pocket. "Good morning Mr. Adamson." He extended his hand.

"How's the family, doctor?" Dad asked.

"Good. Good. The youngest is looking into colleges on the East Coast, so the wife and I will be empty nesters soon."

"Ah, good for you." I thought I saw a glint of bitterness in Dad's eyes before he pressed on. "I need you to examine Wendy to see if she's still intact."

"I'm sorry, sir?"

My heart hit the floor. I shifted uneasily on the table.

"To see if she's still a virgin."

The Mother Fucker! That's why he came in here.

"Sure, sure Mr. Adamson. I can do that, but you're going to have to wait in the lobby during the exam." The doctor's hand was already reaching for the doorknob.

After Dad left the room, Dr. Simon took out his stethoscope and gazed down at it a moment with a pensive expression on his face. When he placed it on the center of my back, I flinched. "Take a deep breath," he said.

The last time I had had an appointment with Dr. Simon it was for my weight. After telling him I hated my body, he had given me a prescription of Preludin, an appetite suppressant that was also a stimulant. Those little pink pills helped me not eat, but eventually it caused my hands to shake so I stopped taking them.

Dr. Simon listened to my lungs and told me to breathe.

"Why do you think your Dad wants you checked out?"

"Probably because I ran away."

"Why did you do that?"

There was a part of me that longed to tell Dr. Simon that I had been wanting to run away ever since I was a little kid. I wanted to tell him it was hard living inside my house. That my family was crazy and that no kid should be subjected to that, but my jaw remained clamped shut.

"Have you had sex with anyone?"

"No. I swear I haven't had sex before."

He moved the stethoscope lower down my back. "Breathe."

My chest expanded as I inhaled.

"This is between you and me, but I'm going to tell your father that I examined you and you're still a virgin."

"Really? You would do that?" On the one hand I believed he was telling me the truth, but it also didn't compute. My experience with adults was they couldn't be trusted, though Dr. Simon seemed quite sincere.

"Yes. I believe you." He shrugged.

"Thank you so much, doctor." I let out a long sigh.

A few minutes later Dad was ushered back into the exam room ready for the news.

"So, Mr. Adamson, I'm glad to report she's still intact."

"Are you sure?" he said, raising an eyebrow.

"Yes. I'm positive."

I couldn't tell if Dad was disappointed because that meant he had been wrong or he didn't trust the doctor, but whatever it was, it added one more thing to my long list of resentments toward him.

Incorrigible

The sky was a slate gray. Cars drove into the lot looking for places to park. A mist was rolling in from the ocean a few blocks away. People shuffled by in a blur as Dad took another hit from his cigarette in front of the double doors of Santa Monica Court House.

We hadn't talked on the drive over, and I couldn't get a read on him. His lips were pulled tight and his eyes were cold and blank. He must hate me. Why shouldn't he? I was the kid who gave him the hard times. The one who cut her wrist. The cause of his late-night trips to the police station.

Another kid in formal clothes passed by us and entered the courthouse. Dad was wearing his button-down shirt and slacks. He snuffed out his cigarette and waved me inside where attorneys in expensive three-piece suits were rushing down the corridor with briefcases in their hands. Uniformed cops and what I suspected were undercover narcs were talking to each other in hushed tones.

I kept my head low and walked a few feet behind Dad. I was embarrassed by his limp. His emaciated polio leg had become an indicator that he, too, was broken. And by then Dad had trained me to hide the family's flaws. When we got to Division A, it was a room overflowing with exhausted parents and a bunch of fuck-ups around my age. I followed my dad up front where we found a couple of seats. My thoughts were buzzing around my head like bees in a jar when everyone in the room stood up as the judge entered wearing his flowing black robes.

After an hour of kids getting called up in front of Judge Thomas, I was beginning to learn the drill. None of the them got a chance to plead guilty or not guilty like I had seen on television. In juvenile court the kids were usually put on probation or asked to come back in six weeks for a progress report. The judge seemed kind of cool and I had convinced myself I would probably get probation when my name was called by the bailiff.

Pushing the bangs out of my face, I followed my dad beyond the sectioned off area to stand side by side behind a long conference table in front of the judge. My mouth was dry and my throat was tight. I shifted my feet as I chewed on my lower lip.

"So, Wendy, it says here, you ran away from home?" Judge Thomas voice was laced with concern.

"Well, sir I, I..."

Dad in all his infinite wisdom about the inner-workings of my mind stepped in to speak.

"Excuse me Your Honor. I would like to say something to the court."

"Yes, Mr. Adamson. Go ahead."

"I honestly don't know what to do with Wendy anymore. She doesn't listen to me and does whatever she wants." His voice was seething with frustration.

There was a moment of silence as Judge Thomas glanced at me.

"Do you think counseling might help?" he asked.

"No. Nothing helps. I can't control her anymore. I give up." My dad raised both his hands and shook them in the air as if he was surrendering.

My fists were clenched so tight the nails were digging into my palms. I lowered my head. Why didn't Dad tell me he was going to do this? How could he throw me under the fucking bus in front of an entire courtroom? I thought I would get probation but he's making it so much worse than it actually is.

Judge Thomas' eyes looked sad as he said, "Unfortunately, I have no choice but to surrender you over to the State of California for being incorrigible. That means you will be taken to juvenile hall today to wait further evaluation from a probation officer."

A wave of panic swept over me. I wanted to plead with my dad. Please don't send me away. Why are you doing this to me? Heart beating, I imagined throwing myself at the mercy of the court. Whatever wall I had around me, my dad had just sealed me in.

A muscular crew-cutted bailiff approached me from behind and led me by the back of the arm around the table. It was clear I wasn't going out the same way I had come in. I was leaving as a stamped criminal out the back exit. The walk seemed long, but when I turned back to look at my dad, the space between us seemed even further. I had no idea what would happen to me now. A thin layer of sweat beaded on my forehead. From a distance, I couldn't tell if the expression on my father's face was sadness or relief.

In that moment I wished he were dead.

Juvie

Sylmar Juvenile Hall is one of three facilities in Los Angeles where the justice system sends teens with behavioral problems. Established in 1965, it was meant only to be temporary housing until a probation officer could figure out placement, but even to this day, teens often stay for months and sometimes even a year. Still, it is considered the best juvie in L.A.

After being processed into Juvie, I was issued stiff sheets, an orange shift and snug white tennis shoes that pinched my feet. My hair was still wet from their shower and I was shivering as an officer ordered me into the 6-by-8-foot room. Its walls were pale yellow cinder block. I took in the surroundings; a bunk bed bolted to the floor, and a small metal desk to my right. That was it. I flinched when the officer slammed the door behind me.

I covered the thin mattress with the sheets and laid down on the bunk. My chest was tangled with fear and rage. I replayed the court scene with my dad over and over again. How could he tell the judge he was done with me? I was his daughter for fucks sake.

I wanted to hurt myself, cut into my body. Any kind of release would do. I dug into my arm with my nails until I fell asleep.

Days passed on the receiving unit until, one day I was drifting off when I heard the sound of a key unlocking the door. "You're being moved to Unit C," the officer said. "Roll up your sheets and set them out here in the hallway."

I didn't want to move to the population. I wanted to be left alone. It was hard to imagine how I'd ever function amongst others. Girls had a way of sensing fear on other girls. But I wasn't being asked, so I did what I was told. A few minutes later I stood at the officer's station when a thick-boned girl with cobalt eyes walked up behind me.

"Am I going back to Unit C-D?" she asked.

"Yup, Rachel. You'll be going with Wendy here." The officer nodded.

Rachel looked me up and down. I responded with a weak smile.

We were led outside where I had to blink back the brightness of the sun. A tall red brick wall with barbed wire surrounded the grass which was the size of a football field. A sidewalk looped around the perimeter connecting several buildings together.

On our walk, Rachel started to talk to me.

"What are you in for?" she asked.

"Runaway," I said. "How about you?"

"Assault and battery."

I wondered who she had assaulted, but not familiar with juvie etiquette, I didn't want to pry.

"Have you been here before?" I asked.

Rachel laughed. "Many times."

We stopped in front of a squat, pale yellow building where we were let into a dayroom packed with girls sitting around. The smell of hormones and sweat hung in the air. All the activity and talking stopped as the girls' heads turn to stare. My stomach was twisted in knots as I tried to avoid direct eye contact.

"Yo, Rachel, you back already?" one girl called.

"I missed you guys." Rachel shrugged.

Laughter broke as we were led away to a small office where chicken-wired windows allowed the officers to keep an eye on things while they did their paperwork. There were two doors on each side of the office with corridors reaching out like arms. Unit C was on one side, and Unit D on the other. An officer in her mid-twenties wearing a tight ponytail sat hunched over a clunky desk.

"I got a couple newbies for you, Murphy," our escort said.

When she stood up, Murphy was built like an athlete, nearly six feet tall.

"Thanks, Sarge," she said.

After the officer left Murphy gave us a quick orientation. "Welcome to Unit-C ladies. Going to give you some of the rules so you'll know how things operate around here."

"I already know the drill," Rachel yawned.

"Seeing how you've put in more hours here than I have, Rachel, you should know the drill."

Rachel jutting out her hip and lifted her chin in a pointless stance of defiance.

"Just so you girls know, I hate doing paperwork." Murphy's brow furrowed. "So, don't give me any reason to write you up." She looked at me, to Rachel and back to me again.

"Yes Ma'am," I said.

"Count times around here are at breakfast, lunch, dinner and before you go to bed. Every evening at 7:30 you will be locked inside your room, so if you need to go to the bathroom make sure to do it beforehand. Oh, and one more thing. There will be absolutely no physical contact. You got that Rachel?"

"Yes ma'am." Rachel clicked her heels and lifted her arm in a salute.

Inside I was smiling but dared not show it on my face.

Murphy handed us both a paper bag stocked with a toothbrush, tooth powder, a small bar of soap, a notepad, a pencil and three stamps, then we were assigned to rooms.

I had just finished making my bunk when I heard Murphy's voice booming down the hall. "Line it up for dinner ladies."

I made my way to the dayroom where I found the girls lined up in twos in front of the door. Rachel saw me and grabbed my arm, "You can be my partner."

I sighed in relief.

My eyes couldn't help but land on a girl with hair slicked back and a shakily drawn neck tattoo who stood closer to the front of the line. I stared. She looked so much like a boy. When she caught me, I looked away. I needed to be more careful or I could get my ass kicked. I just felt it.

Murphy walked up and unlocked the door. "Stay in twos everyone and keep your voices down to a whisper," she said as we were let outside.

The cafeteria was lined with rows of tables with attached stools. I smelled onions and disinfectant. Trays with macaroni & cheese, canned green beans, bread and a small carton of milk were set up waiting for us. I grabbed one and followed Rachel.

We had twenty minutes to eat. All you could hear were spoons dinging on metal trays as we shoved everything into our mouths. I was hungry and swallowed the food barely taking a breath between each bite. When our time was up, we were escorted back to the unit before the next unit came to eat.

After dinner was free time. The dayroom became loud with shrill voices bouncing of the walls. I sat down on a bench to watch everyone. Black girls braided each other's hair. White girls played a card game in one corner. I studied their behaviors like a scientist observing animals in the wild. Something primal in me knew I would have to adapt to this new environment if I wanted to survive.

*

Sunday was always visiting day in juvie. Two weeks into my stay the officer told me that my Dad had called to say he was coming to see me. Well, it's about time, I thought. I bet he can't sleep at night while his daughter is in here rotting away.

After lunch we were locked inside our rooms during visiting hours. I was jittery. I had convinced myself that Dad would probably ask for forgiveness for what he had done. In my mind I was ready to let it go if he'd let me come back home. I was pacing back and forth having a conversation with Dad inside my head when the door opened.

"You have a visitor, Wendy," the officer said.

I took a deep breath and made my way down the hall. There were other girls visiting with their families in the dayroom. Dad sat in the corner wearing one of his white work shirts and loose pants. My feelings were all jumbled. While I was relieved to see him, I didn't want him to know it. Instead, I lowered myself into the chair across from him with my jaw clenched tight.

"How you doing, Pooh?" Dad started calling me that when I was five years old. The nickname came from the Winnie the Pooh book. It used to make me feel so special, but on that particular visiting day, not so much.

"Why did you put me in here?" I narrowed my eyes.

"Me? You put your own self in here."

"You told the judge I was out of control." It was impossible for me to have a simple conversation with my father. Our relationship was littered with emotional landmines and booby trapped with past resentments and blame. His logic made no sense to me. I knew I could be a pain in the ass at times, but I felt justified in my behavior.

"What did you expect me to do, Wendy?" He held up his palms.

"You wanted me out of your house, is all." I figured I was an embarrassment to him. I always had been an embarrassment. And our family life had always consisted of concealing the scandalous facts. First mom's mental illness, then Jay's rage and now it was me.

"Look, Wendy, I don't want to spend my time wondering if you're going to die out there or not." Dad's brow was creased like a paper fan.

"I wasn't going to die." He didn't know I felt dead inside.

"You don't know what's going to happen when you get in cars with strange men."

I never considered my dad's feelings when I didn't come home at night. I just wanted to live in a world where adults didn't tell me what to do all the time.

"Can I come home, Dad? Please? I promise I won't run away again."

Dad was not one to show his emotions, but I thought I saw a glint of sadness behind his eyes, before he changed the subject. "I brought you some of your favorite candy. I gave them to the officer to check them in."

"It's horrible in here. I want to come home."

His red-rimmed eyes darted around the room studying the other families. A Latina woman was holding her daughter's hand, grasped in both of hers. The girl had straight black hair and tears were rolling down her cheeks. It was a tender display of affection, one I wished my dad could make. "It doesn't look so bad in here," he said.

"The girls are fucking scary."

"Has anyone tried to hurt you?"

"No." I thought back to the girl I had ridden over with in the van after court. She was huge and looked mean as a rabid dog. I thought she would kick my ass if given half a chance. "But they might."

His chest heaved as he took a deep breath. His once dark hair had a shock of gray in the front. His face was covered in deep lines. When did Dad start looking so old?

"Please, let me come home." I used my softest tone. I desperately wanted to be in my own room watching television. I wanted to be cocooned under newly washed sheets and cozy blankets in my own bed eating Oreo cookies whenever I wanted to.

Silence.

"I'll go to school, do my homework and do my chores. I'll even stay inside. I promise Dad. Please." I wanted to be a normal girl like the ones who went to my school. To be satisfied with cramming for an algebra exam the night before. I wanted to stop getting in trouble. I just didn't know how.

"Please..."

"It's out of my hands now, Wendy. A probation officer will be coming to see you this week to decide where we go from here."

I leaned back and scowled at him. How could he just give me up like that? Aren't fathers supposed to stand by their daughters no matter what? "You mean where I go from here? We are not going anywhere."

"What did you think would happen, Wendy? You're my daughter, and it is my job to protect you."

I bit my lower lip. I wasn't the type to 'give in' just because my Dad told me "no." I could be relentless if it meant getting my way. I remember the time he grounded me for two weeks for drinking and, I pleaded, "Please Dad let me go out, I promise I won't do it ever again." He eventually lifted the restriction because he got tired of listening to me beg. All I had to do was wear him down long enough so he would cave. But sitting there in juvie, I knew it was a waste of time to beg for my freedom now. After becoming a ward of the court, the rules of the game had suddenly changed. I would have to adjust my tactics, but I didn't know what that meant just yet.

I eyed the open pack of Camels peeking out the front of his shirt pocket and nodded toward them. "Can I have some smokes, then?"

"You're not allowed to smoke in here."

"The girls do it all the time," I whispered, leaning forward.

"But you'll get in trouble if you get caught."

"I won't get caught."

"What if the officer smells the smoke?"

"I can do it inside my room when no one is around."

His eyes darted toward the officer's station. I could sense he was beginning to crack. "Please Dad." I tilted my head sideways and pleaded with my eyes.

When his hand slowly reached for the pack, I felt a sense of victory. If he wasn't going to help me get out of there, I'd use his guilt for a smaller ask. He tapped four cigarettes out and passed them to me down low along with some matches. I quickly tucked them inside my bra.

"Thanks Dad. How's Diane?"

"She's doing okay." He shrugged.

"I bet she's glad I'm gone and she has the room all to herself?"

"I think she misses you," he said, not sounding convincing.

"Sure. At least she'll stop bitching about me wearing her clothes."

"You borrow them without asking."

"That's what sisters do."

Diane was still pissed off at me for getting a cigarette burn on one of her favorite blouses. I don't even remember doing it but I may have been a little drunk at the time. I don't know exactly when Diane started acting distant and cold to me, but I think it's when I got kicked out of St. Monica's and all her friends found out. At that point, I'm sure she was ashamed to have a loser sister who was a huge disgrace in Catholic school.

"Can you bring me some more smokes next week?"

"Not making any promises."

I slid down low in my chair and crossed my arms over my chest. Dad liked me to beg, so at least his little girl would need something from him, even if it was just a cigarette.

After Dad and I said our good-byes, I was locked back inside my room. My palms were sweating and my heart was racing as I lit up the cigarette. I beat back the spiraling smoke with my hand. The red cherry flickered. The harsh smoke burned the back of my throat. I savored the dizziness that came over me. I took another hit and held it in even longer. Sneaking cigarettes gave me a taste of freedom. It was a way of saying to the world: lock me up, but I'm still going to do whatever I want. In the end, it's my life, and I have the ultimate control.

*

Later that day I sat in the dayroom. I was bobbing my head along with the Supremes as Gwen danced across the dayroom floor. Her frame was lean, skin was the color of almonds. Her back was long and erect while her arms pumped expressively by her sides. As she moved it was like a sigh being released from some place deep within her. Each step full of energy, but she showed mastery and control like I had never seen before.

Growing up, I loved watching musicals like The Damn Yankees, West Side Story and Oklahoma. I was intrigued by movement as a means of expression, and more than anything else-I wanted to be able to dance like that.

Ardell was a girl I had met in my first two weeks there. We had talked several times, small exchanges of little consequence, but I found her friendlier than most of the girls. She came and sat down next to me on the bench.

"How was your visit with your dad?" she asked.

We all knew each other's business in there.

"Okay, but he's not going to help me get me out of here." I shrugged.

"At least he came to see you."

"Do your parents come?"

"My dad left when I was three, and my mom is way too busy with a new boyfriend to tear herself away."

"That's a bummer."

While I empathized with Ardell, I had the unique ability to compare other people's experiences to my own. Mathematically, any hardships endured always left my side of the equation in the red. Through a lens of victimhood, no one would ever measure up to my suffering, but just the same it gave me a direct link to their pain.

"Gwen can really dance, can't she?" Ardell nodded her way.

Dancing around with her dyed hair, Gwen was the queen of the dayroom. She ruled the music and therefore controlled the mood of the room.

"I've never seen anyone move like that before," I said. "Do you know the dance she's doing?"

"It's the cha cha. I've been doing it since I was five years old."

All I was doing at five was dancing around my mother's suicide attempts or navigating my father's drunkenness.

"I can show you how to do it." Ardell suddenly stood up and I was looking up at her face.

"Oh hell naw, girl." I leaned back.

"I thought you wanted to learn?"

"Well yeah, but when no one else is around."

"When do you think that might be?"

"Um, I guess you have a point."

Ardell tugged my arm. "Come on," she said.

"Alright alright." I stood up.

"Just do what I do."

We stood shoulder to shoulder. And while I had been doing a pretty good job staying under the radar, I was feeling others watching me now. I stared down at my feet to avoid any embarrassing eye contact. I thought if no one noticed me I would be able to avoid conflicts.

The only problem was in such small quarters, one can't help but notice you.

"Left foot forward-and-left-foot-back. One-two-cha cha cha. Right foot back-then-right-foot-forward. One two cha-cha-cha." Ardell moved slowly and methodically as she explained the dance.

When I made an attempt to follow my feet wouldn't cooperate.

"Just get the basic steps down first," she said, in a patient tone.

"I'm so retarded. I don't think I can do it." I pounded my thigh with a tight fist.

Ardell was persistent. "One-two, cha-cha-cha. Say it inside your head." She snapped her fingers, indicating how to keep the rhythm in mind.

"I can't do it." Aware that Gwen was watching us now, I moved toward the bench. I wasn't about to look like a fool in front of everyone.

"We can practice again tomorrow if you want," Ardell said.

"Yeah. Okay."

I was so grateful for Ardell's kindness I wanted to do something to pay her back. "Want to go in my room and smoke?"

"Really? You have some?"

"Meet me there." I got up and rushed down the corridor.

A few minutes later I was standing behind the door holding a cigarette between my fingers when Ardell slid in. My back was pressed against the cool cinder-block wall, my foot tapping as I struck the match. Once it was lit, I brought the cigarette to my lips and took a hit. Ardell fanned her hand over the spiraling smoke. I exhaled upward and then passed her the cigarette. Her chest heaved as she took a drag. "I feel dizzy," she said.

"Me too." We both laughed. The excitement of being sneaky skyrocketed the adrenaline through my veins. The rush of nicotine helped me forget that fact that I wasn't going home.

*

I started to envision doing the cha-cha in my mind. I imagined it before drifting off to sleep or while I was supposed to be doing assignments in school. I was determined to learn, so Ardell started giving me lessons in the corridor, away from the other girls." One, two, cha-cha-cha" became my mantra.

After several weeks, I was able to do the basic moves, but still lacked any real style or grace. That didn't stop me from practicing in my room. The more I did it the more my body limbered up. Eventually, after a lot of work, I was ready to take my dancing moves center stage.

"You sure you're ready for this?" Ardell asked.

"As ready as I'll ever be."

Standing in the dayroom, Ardell and I stood facing each other as dance partners. Other girls were absorbed in conversations or playing cards. Gwen was lost in her own dance, and not paying any attention to us.

"Remember to start with the right leg," Ardell said, patting her thigh.

I nodded and took a deep breath.

The song You're My Everything by The Temptations came on. Ardell came toward me, and my right leg went back, hitting the ground with a slight bounce. My hips swayed like well-oiled pistons. All the practice, all the repetition paid off. I may have tripped up once or twice, but I was quickly able to get back in sync with Ardell. My arms loosened up. I could feel the eyes of other girls looking up from what they were doing to watch. This time, I kept my head up, reveling in the attention. I had done the work and my body was a testament to that. A thin layer of sweat beaded up on my flesh. A smile spread across my face. A taut breath was liberated from my chest. For a girl who always felt invisible in a room, dancing made me feel like I was being seen, and therefore made me feel alive.

*

I studied the girls in juvie more closely than any textbook I was required to read in school. I watched them as if they were all actors in a movie. How they moved. The way they laughed. Their hand gestures as they spoke and the things they said like "Sho nuff" and "You ain't lying, girl." Juvenile hall had its own language and I was determined to learn it as fast as I could. More than anything, I wanted them to like me, but I knew I had to fit in first. My survival depended on it.

The more I observed, the more certain I was that Gwen was the queen. It wasn't by force, either, but by the way she carried herself. She was the embodiment of ever-elusive, confidence and cool, but it didn't hurt that she could dance her ass off to any song. I was determined to align myself with Gwen.

"Yo," I said, when I entered the dayroom. "What's happening, Gwen?"

"You know." Her front tooth glimmered with gold.

Measuring my words carefully, I said, "I can dig it girl."

Gwen started dancing and soon, I was dancing along with other girls. Smokey Robinson's voice was coming out of the small record player in the corner. Gwen owned the floor taking up a lot of space, and everyone made sure to get out of her way. I started to sense someone's eyes on me. A new girl with two inches of black roots on top of her blond hair was staring. There was something in Blondie's face that looked like contempt, but I convinced myself she must be jealous because of the way I moved. It was the sixties and as oblivious as I was to prejudice, there was racial tension that still lingered from the Watts riots from the year before.

At first, I ignored her, and focused on gliding with the beat of the music. That is, until Gwen said something that would change all that.

"That new girl keeps giving you hard looks." Gwen nodded in Blondie's direction.

"What's her problem anyway?" My eyes became slits.

"She obviously doesn't like you."

"What the fuck is up with that?"

"If it were me, I'd ask her what she's staring at."

Gwen had clearly challenged me. It might have been my imagination, but it felt like everyone in the dayroom was watching to see what I would do. If this were a movie, this would be the time everything in the background fades away and the camera would zoom directly into my face. I had never been a fighter, saving that feature for the guys I chose, but this moment could define me for the rest of my stay. If I handled it correctly, it would earn me the right kind of juvie reputation I would need in order to survive.

My heart raced. My breath was shallow. Queen Gwen was glaring at me with a questioning eyebrow. I couldn't see any other option. I puffed out my chest and strutted over to Blondie on the other side of the room. I stood two feet directly in front of her, placed my hands on my hips and said, "What seems to be the problem girl?"

Blondie's lip curled in disgust. "Why don't you go back and boogie-woogie with your friends over there?" she said, waving me away like I was a gnat.

The camera would have done another close-up to capture all the pent-up rage behind my eyes. There might have been a montage of flash backs to Sister Mary Magdalena, Irene, my dad, and everyone else who had ever come at me. Not about to lose my hard earned-cha-cha cred, I was considering how this might go down. How big of a leap was it really, from dancing to fighting? I wondered where her most vulnerable places on her body might be. Should I go for the throat or do a body slam? My face grew hotter and hotter. My hands began to shake.

At this point the camera would have done a panoramic sweep of all the wide-eyed girls in the dayroom until it finally landed on Gwen, who said, "You gonna let that bitch get away with that?" Her booming voice drowned out everything else.

The camera would have caught the rage that flashed across my face right before I leaped.

There was a hollow smack as Blondie and I hit the ground with a force that caused my breath to jack-knife in my chest. My fingers instinctively went for her dark roots until pieces of it came off in my hands. Blondie's torso lurched upward. We rolled across the dayroom floor in a tangled heap of flailing arms and legs. It only took seconds before I found myself on top pinning her down while the girls gathered around.

"Kick the bitch's ass."

"Hit her! Hit her!" another voice yelled.

At this point, the camera would zoom in on the trickle of blood coming out of her nose. It would catch a flash of surprise from behind her eyes, my hands pinning her wrists to the concrete floor as red welts appeared across her arm. The noise grew to a roar, attracting the day officer, who grabbed me by the elbows and pulled me off.

Camera cuts to the dayroom door where two more officers barge in.

"You're going to lock-up now," one of them said.

"What? No way."

I was quickly ushered outside. My head was spinning as the burly officer let go of my arm and asking, "What the hell was that all about?"

"It was her fault." I pushed the hair away from my face.

"It's always that way with you girls." She shook her head.

Moments later I was being led down a hallway to the dreaded infirmary.

"Welcome to lock-up, Missy," the officer said, directing me inside a room.

I flinched when she slammed the door behind me. As I stood there looking around at the silver toilet, the small sink, the adrenaline was pumping through my veins. I paced back and forth while cursing the bitch out loud.

All of a sudden it struck me that all the fight actually got me was being put in lock-up. A feeling of dread settled in my chest. And then the familiar self-hatred began to rise up in me for being so stupid. Why am I trying to win people over? Those girls could care less about you. What the fuck's wrong with you anyway?

Everything fades to black.

*

During my time in lock-up I got an unexpected visit. An officer unlocked my door and said, "Someone is here to see you."

"Who is it?"

"I have no idea but get your dress on."

I changed from my night gown into my orange county shift. After I put my shoes on, she escorted me to the administration offices where a woman with short permed hair and a body shaped like a barrel sat at a small table.

"Have a seat," she said. "Hello Wendy. My name is Mrs. Shelton and I'm your probation officer."

"Oh?"

"I need to ask you some questions."

"Yes ma'am." I shrugged.

"How long have you been doing drugs?"

"I've just smoked a little pot a couple times," I lied.

"You were arrested with drug dealers who were selling cocaine in the Valley."

"Oh them? They picked us up hitchhiking. I didn't know what they did."

"Look Wendy, can we just be real here?"

"I am." I tried my best to feign innocence.

She asked me a series of intrusive questions and took notes. About Dad, my siblings and my home life. I'm sure I squirmed a bit as it was making me real uncomfortable. When she was done shooting off her questions, Mrs. Shelton set her pen down on the table.

"So, let me tell you what happens next, Wendy. You are going to a foster home."

"Why can't I go back home?"

"You don't follow the rules at home, so we are going to try something new."

"But, but, I don't want to..."

"It's not what you want anymore, Wendy. You are a ward of the court now and I will be making the decisions from here on out." I bit down hard on my bottom lip so I wouldn't say something stupid that I would regret, but in my mind I cussed her out. She gathered up her papers and slipped them into a briefcase. "I'll be picking you up when I find a suitable home."

"So that's it?"

"I'm afraid so."

As I walked back to lock up, my fists were balled up.
I couldn't believe a complete stranger was making decisions in my life and I had no say-so in the matter. I
thought back to Camarillo when Patty and Terry were
made to go back to juvenile hall. I was beginning to understand how scared and alone they must have felt. My
life was no longer my own.

Foster Care

La Puente was a barrio, populated by mostly Spanish speaking, low-income families thirty miles east of Los Angeles. As Mrs. Shelton drove down the main boulevard, I paid close attention to the details, getting more pissed off with every block. I couldn't believe she was taking me to a foster home nowhere near a beach.

"This looks kind of ghetto," I said, squinting at some cholo looking guys drinking beer on the lawn.

"It's better than juvenile hall," she snapped.

I rolled my eyes. Juvie wasn't all that bad. I had made a lot of friends and learned how to do the Cha-Cha.

A few minutes later we pulled up into a nicer neighborhood, but not by much. She parked in front of a brown stucco with a manicured lawn. I grabbed the small garbage bag with my belongings and followed Mrs. Shelton up the path. A beefy woman topped by black curly hair and rolls of pasty flesh for a neck greeted us at the door. "You must be Wendy," she said, throwing her arms around me. Her embrace made me squirm.

"Yes, Mariam," Mrs. Shelton said. "And... she is extremely happy to be here. Aren't you Wendy?"

"Yes ma'am," I said, my voice muffled inside Mariam's thick flesh.

"Welcome, welcome," Mariam said. "Come on in."

"I'm afraid I can't stay. I have another kid that I have to pick up and take back to juvenile hall today." I figured that she was saying that for my benefit. "If you have any problems be sure to call me." She handed Mariam her business card before she left. And there I was, in La Puente in my new home, with strangers.

Mariam and I stepped into the living room she introduced me to her two dogs. One was a small white poodle named Fluff that yelped shrilly at my feet. The other was a brown Dachshund, named Susie, who had a pot belly that nearly touched the floor.

"The vet put Susie on a diet this week," Mariam said, struggling to lean over to pat Susie's head. "So we don't give her any food, even if she's begging."

The smell of baked bread and savory roast drifted in from the kitchen. I took a deep breath, looking forward to a home-cooked meal, instead of the starchy food that they served in juvie.

The place looked like a typical grandma's house. Porcelain figurines everywhere. White crocheted doilies that I figured Mariam had made with her pudgy fingers covered most of the furniture. A television sat in the center of the room with a big leather recliner directly in front of it. Shelves and glass cabinets held animal statuettes and wide-eyed Precious Moments dolls. Soon, I'd learn that Mariam found some secret satisfaction from arranging, re-arranging, and dusting these little figurines. For me, it would just mean more work.

"Tell me a little about yourself Wendy," Mariam said, as we sat on the brown tweed couch. "What grade are you in now?"

"8th grade," I said. "But I'm behind on my credits."

"That's okay, dearie. You'll have plenty of time to catch up."

Plenty of time? I'd be there a couple months, maximum.

"You can call me Mom if you like."

I felt my throat close up. No, no, no. That was a no-fly zone for me. When I didn't answer, she finally said, "Or you can call me Mariam. Whichever you like."

I responded with a weak smile and reached over to pet Susie who was stationed by my feet.

"You have two foster sisters. They will be getting home shortly and they are very excited to meet you." Mariam said. "Darlene is your age and she also came from juvenile hall. And Nancy is nineteen. We met her at church." Mariam paused.

"I don't know if Mrs. Shelton told you, but we're Mormon, ya know?"

"Oh, great," I said, swallowing hard.

As far as I was concerned, religion was a load of crap. I'd given up on God a long time ago. My mom had been a devout Catholic and look where it had gotten her. As for Mormons, all I knew about them was they seemed to always be prepping for the end of the world. I'd heard they stock piled loads of supplies and food. I gazed out the sliding glass door to the backyard to see if there were any visible bunkers.

Mariam chattered on and I nodded and smiled. It was only a few minutes later until Nancy came bouncing in the front door. She was warm, with long blond hair, a moon face and green eyes that shone with flecks of amber. I liked her immediately. Sitting down on the couch next to me, Nancy told me about her boyfriend, Ron, whom she had met at church. She beamed as she explained how they were getting married after he was done serving his term with the Marines.

"Nancy is in the church choir," Mariam said, brimming with pride. "Just wait till you hear her play the piano."

When the door flew open again, it was Darlene. She was practically jumping up and down when she saw me. "Oh my God, I'm so happy to meet you." She pulled me up by the wrist to give me a hug. All this touching was too much for me.

Darlene had a beaverish overbite, and stiff crunchy hair that smelled of Aqua Net. Unlike with Nancy, my internal defenses activated. I knew she was fake.

"Darlene, would you show Wendy to the room?" Mariam said.

"Of course," she picked up my bag. "Let me help you with your things."

I followed Darlene down a narrow hallway past gold, framed photos of the family. Across the hall from the master was our bedroom that we shared. There were twin beds with floral chenille spreads and two identical dressers. Darlene dropped the bag onto the furthest bed.

"This is where you'll sleep." Her tone changed from perky to flat.

I started to put what few belongings I had into the drawers. Panties, socks, a pair of shorts. The last time I saw my dad in juvie, he had said he'd be coming to visit me and would bring me more clothes. When I tried to talk him into letting me come home, he told me again, that it was out of his hands.

"What got you here?" Darlene laid out across her bed, leaning up on her elbow.

"Getting high and running away," I said.

"Same here." Darlene nodded. "Just wait till you meet Mike. Your new foster father."

"What do you mean?"

"Oh, he's from the bible belt. He hates everyone."

*

The entire family had to sit down for Mariam's dinners.

"This is Wendy, Mike," Mariam said. His hair was still wet from taking a shower when he got home from work.

Mike had gray hair, a square jaw, and tight lips that looked like a line drawn across his face. He gave me an awkward, stiff hug. "Welcome, young lady."

We all sat around the table covered with a tablecloth patterned with twisting grapevines.

"She's a pretty one, Mariam," he said.

"Yes, honey. I know."

Mariam, put a plate in front of me–pot roast, mashed potatoes, and gravy. I was starving and ate like I hadn't eaten in days.

I don't remember what we talked about that first night, but I do remember being shocked by Mike's use of the N-word. Up until that point I had never seen anyone hate another based on the color of their skin. His dinner rant involved the Fair Housing Act of 1968 that passed that same year, just after Martin Luther King's assassination. Mike was afraid it would change the color of his neighborhood.

"If those damn niggers move in, I'm moving back home, Mariam," he said.

"Yes, honey," Mariam said.

I could tell he was a powder keg with a hair trigger, so Mariam would have to agree with him. Once the dishes were cleared, he retreated to the living room, his feet shooting out in front of him as he reclined on the lazy boy chair.

"Play something for us, would ya Nance?" he said.

"Sure, Daddy," Nancy said, lowering herself in front of the shiny Steinway.

I watched from the couch as Nancy bowed her head. She paused, before her hands lifted. As she played her fingers danced across the black and white keys so lightly, they reminded me of butterflies. As soon as that first note hit my ears, I let out a soft sigh. The sound was so precise, it hung in the air like a cloud. I looked over at Mike and all his anger from moments before seemed to melt away. The corners of his lips curled up in a smile.

I loved hearing Nancy play, but it magnified all my failures. I'd been given the opportunity to succeed at anything, anywhere. I took piano lessons, but quit. I also quit tap dance, ballet and art classes. I'd succeeded at becoming a seasoned quitter.

More evidence that there was something wrong with me.

*

Several months into my stay I was propped up on my pillow, reading The Shining in my room. Darlene was on the bed across from me. By then it had become crystal clear that the two of us had little in common. She was always trying to kiss up to our foster parents and I found it quite annoying. But the one thing that we did have in common was both of us dreaded the weekly Missionary visits. For some reason, the Millers felt it was their obligation to save our souls, so they enlisted missionaries to come to the house every week to talk to us.

"Girls, you have visitors," Mariam yelled from the other room.

"Oh, fuck!" Darlene said.

"Shit!" I slammed my book closed and pushed myself up off the bed.

When we entered the living room the same fresh-faced guys, Jeff and George extended their hands to greet us. Their cheeks were still flushed from the bike ride over, the only means of transportation they were allowed to use. Mariam smiled before disappearing into the kitchen to finish baking cookies.

"Good to see you girls again," Jeff said.

They both had crew cuts, black dress pants, white shirts and ties. This was the standard uniform for missionaries who devoted years of their lives trying to convert people over to their religion.

Darlene and I down sat down on the couch. The men—boys really--- sat across from us in straight-back dining room chairs. "Have you girls given any more thought to what we talked about last week?" George said.

I resisted the urge to roll my eyes straight to heaven.

"I told you I don't believe in that stuff." Darlene crossed her arms over her chest.

"You're familiar with the gospel?" Jeff asked.

"Ah...yeah. I went to Catholic school." I wanted to let him know I was no dummy.

"Then you know that our Father in heaven sent his son, Jesus Christ, in order to save us all from sin?"

Darlene released an audible sigh. "Can I ask you something?"

They both leaned forward eager to answer our questions. "Of course."

"How do you even know God is real?" Darlene asked.

"I have faith," George said.

"Faith in what exactly?" I asked.

He paused briefly, then said, "When I was 21-years-old I was struggling and fell away from God. But when I read the 'word' I learned that the prophet, Joseph Smith, had a revelation that substances separate us from the love of God." He leaned forward, brow furrowed, his hands on his knees. "So, I decided to test my faith, by giving up alcohol, coffee, tobacco to see if the scripture were actually true. Lo and behold, I started to have more clarity and came to believe in God again."

"But you were biased when you took the test," I said.

"What do you mean?"

"As a Mormon, didn't you want these things to be true?"

"What I'm trying to say is, if you pray to God, He will testify to you in His own way as well."

"Someone once testified against me in court and that didn't go so well," Darlene said.

I smiled.

Jeff was unfazed. He opened his book and pointed to a yellow highlighted page. "Let me read you a little parable."

We both stared blankly through him.

"Mathew 7:24-27 says: Everyone then who hears these words of mine and does them will be like a wise man who built his house on the rock. And the rain fell, and the floods came and the winds blew and beat on that house, but it did not fall, because had been founded his house on a rock. And it's a foolish man who built his house on the sand. And the rain fell, and the floods came, and the winds blew, and great was the fall of it."

"So, God supposedly loves everyone, unless you live at the beach?" I asked.

George looked away. It was pointless. We were from different planets.

After they left, Darlene and I went back to our room. While we didn't agree on a lot of things, on that day, Darlene and I wrapped our pinkies around one another and swore that come hell or high water, we'd never convert.

Time passed quickly in foster care. I was doing better in school. My dad visited me on the weekends. Things seemed to be moving in the right direction for me to one day go back home. And then something changed at dinner one night.

"I've got some good news," Darlene said.

"What's that, dear?" Mariam asked.

"I'm converting to the Mormon church."

"Oh my, Darlene that is wonderful news." Mariam held a pudgy hand over her heart.

My fork stopped midway to my mouth. "You what?"

I couldn't believe it. This was a shock. We had sworn, and she had broken our vow. Later in our room I confronted her. "You said we weren't going to convert no matter what."

"Jeff and George changed my mind." She shrugged.

"You just want to kiss Millers' asses."

"I've had an awakening, and maybe that's something you just can't understand."

Darlene's head hit the pillow, her curly hair fanning out as she turned to face the wall. I threw daggers at her with my eyes. She had betrayed me and I wanted revenge. I wasn't sure how that would happen, but I'd watch and wait for an opportunity to pay her back.

*

Two weeks later I woke up to the sound of rain battering the roof. I heard noise coming from the living room and went to explore. I found Mariam crying and Buddy pacing back and forth. Darlene came in just behind me. "What's wrong?" I asked.

"Sit down girls. We have something to tell you," Mariam said. Her chest heaved as she took a deep breath. "Nancy and Ron were in an accident.

Oh my God. What happened?" I asked

Mariam explained how Nancy had driven with Ron to Camp Pendleton to get another pass. Due to poor visibility, someone had entered the freeway the wrong way and crashed into them. A head-on collision. I swallowed a lump in the back of my throat.

"Ron is dead." Tears were streaming down Mariam's cheeks. "And we don't know if Nancy is going to make it."

Not Nancy. Please not her.

Here it was again. Nothing ever turned out right. Not just for me, but for anyone I ever loved. More evidence in my airtight case that God was a load of crap.

Mariam and Buddy left to the hospital. In the afternoon I stared at the television in a trance. It wasn't until early evening the phone finally rang. I looked over at Darlene before I got up to answer it.

"She's stable now," Mariam said, from the other end. "But it's still touch-and-go."

When I hung up I told Darlene the news. All the resentment over her betrayal had disappeared. Instead, we hugged and sobbed with relief. I may not have realized it then, but for the first time in my life, someone else's tragedy had dwarfed my own.

For the next three months the Millers were at the hospital every day while Darlene and I picked up the slack around the house by doing extra chores. We would get updates on the countless surgeries Nancy had. At first the doctors didn't know if she'd ever be able to walk again, and then the feelings came back to her legs. Then they didn't know if her vision would be restored, until weeks in she was able to see again. The doctors started to refer to Nancy as a miracle girl. But with all the reports we got from the Millers, nothing could have prepared me for that first visit to her hospital room.

When I walked in, Nancy was propped up in bed with a shaved head, skinny, all hard edges and protruding bones. Her eyes had been knocked loose on impact, and it looked like they had been put back in the sockets wrong. Her teeth were lined with silver braces. A jagged scar ran across her forehead where her eyebrows had been. I was overpowered by a strong odor of sickness and ammonia. It felt like I couldn't breathe.

"Don't be scared," Nancy said. "It's still me in here."

I tried to smile, but I couldn't. "I'll be right back."

I was nauseous and walked down the corridor until I came to a water fountain and vomited inside it. Embarrassment slithered up my spine. I wanted to show Nancy my support and my love, but the mere sight of her had made me sick.

Six months after the accident, Nancy was finally released. I remember feeling awkward and not knowing what to say to make her feel better. But one day Nancy surprised me when she began to play her gorgeous music at the piano.

How the hell does she do it? How does she go on after everything that has happened to her?

And then as we were sitting together on the couch, she explained to me how she was able to keep going.

"I'm at peace with everything."

"Really?"

"Oh, I still miss Ronny alright, but when I was in the operating room, an angel came to my side and told me not to worry because he was going to be okay."

I examined her face, the scars that ran along her delicate, pale skin, and the dark circles under her eyes. "And you believed this, this, angel?"

"I choose to believe," she said, meeting my gaze.

I didn't understand it back then, but all these years later, I realize it was just that simple for Nancy. She chose to believe in something greater than herself, and it gave her the ability to go on. I would blame God for everything in my life, and that gave me a reason to self-destruct.

I don't remember why but a few months later I left that foster home and went to one in San Pedro, where I stayed a month. Finally, Dad talked to my P.O. and they both agreed to let me come back home to see how I'd behave.

Mad Max

Max blew into my life like one of those Bad Boys, bringing with him the illusion of security. I was sixteen hanging out at the Santa Monica pier. Laura and I sat on the railing, smoking and watching the procession of girls in bikini and boys in board shorts stroll by. Sweat dripped down the small of my back. The smell of hot dogs and cotton candy drifted from the nearby food stands. All of the sudden my eyes landed on Max, a gorgeous Latino boy I knew only by reputation. He swaggered towards us, bare chested, hip hugger jeans and a white t-shirt tucked in his back pocket. My heart raced like a trapped bird was caught inside my chest.

"Hey Max, what's happening?" Laura said.

I sat there kicking my feet as they talked. I couldn't help but stare at his high cheekbones, big brown eyes and black wavy hair. When Max smiled and asked for my number, of course I gave it to him.

Our first real date, if you can call it that, was a Halloween party where Max dressed up as a hooker and I went as a gypsy. The party was fun and I was beaming with pride to be on Max's arm. But just as we were leaving, a guy dressed in a cowboy suit grabbed my ass. Max punched him in the jaw, causing him to tumble backwards and crash into a glass aquarium, spilling tropical fish on the floor. While this may have been a red flag for some girls, for me, it was a flashing neon light saying, I'm your guy.

For the next six months Max and I were inseparable. My school attendance dropped, but I managed not to get caught as I had mastered the craft of forging my dad's signature. On many weekdays Max would pick me across from Santa Monica High School. We went to every party together. We took the bus together. When we walked, he laced my hand through the crook of his arm and positioned himself near the street to protect me from the elements. He'd open doors for me. Lit my cigarettes. Never in my life had I been treated like that. Max was a spigot of fresh water in my otherwise dry and cracked wasteland.

Since Max liked to get high as much as I did, I took it as another sign our relationship was pre-destined. Max's best friend, Adam, was having a party at his house. Adam was a football player with dark black hair, a baby face and a barrel of a body. After a trip he took to Hawaii, Adam liked to wear white puka shells, even though it looked like they could pop right off his thick neck.

When we arrived at the party, Adam's living room was already filled with a cloud of smoke that hovered below the ceiling. Some of the people were new friends I had inherited from being Max's girlfriend, others I knew from St Monica's. Patty was one from the latter category. She wore a clinging cheetah-patterned top and always seemed to have one eye on Max, while I had one eye on her.

Max opened a wine cooler from the fridge and handed it to me. I looked up at his flawless almond skin and big brown eyes and smiled.

"You're so fine," he said, kissing me on the lips.

I lowered my head. I wasn't used to getting compliments.

While Max moved about the room socializing, I sat in an oversized chair where I could watch. Santana's Black Magic Woman thumped from the stereo, and loud laughter bounced off the walls. The party was already in full swing when Mitch, a stoner dude, held up a small baggy full of pills and shook it in the air. "Party favors anyone?"

"Homie, homie-don't you know me?" Max approached him with one hand already extended.

Nearly everyone took one of those pills and popped them into their mouths, and of course, I did the same. It didn't even occur to me to ask what it was. But I would find out a few minutes later I had taken Purple Owsley, named after Owsley Stanley, who had invented one the purest forms of LSD long before the Summer of Love.

An hour later, I started feeling the effects. My fingers tingled and my tongue went numb. There was a buzzing vibration inside my chest. It felt warm and similar to infatuation, but not the boy-crush I was used to. Everyone seemed to be moving in slow motion. Laughter and voices echoed like we were inside an underground tunnel. My entire body started to vibrate. My back, my neck, my nose, my big toes, my armpits, nipples, belly and down to the hairs on my calves. When I moved the cigarette toward my mouth my hand left a trail behind it. When I looked at Max, he was animated and standing in the doorway of the kitchen making people laugh. It was getting late and I wanted to tell him I needed to get home because my probation officer was always on my case. I was trying hard not to do anything that might result in going back to juvie and being away from Max. Finally, I'd found a reason to stay out of trouble--or at least not get caught. My legs felt heavy and I couldn't figure out how to maneuver from the chair to tell Max I had to go.

As Adam shot photos of us all that night, I managed to push myself out of the oversized chair to tell Max I had to get home There was still time to catch the last bus that would take me to my neighborhood across town, a neighborhood where they didn't have parties mixed with Latinos and whites.

"I'll walk you to the bus stop," Max said.

We crossed Ocean Park Boulevard to Sixth Street, just as the bus was coming down the street. Max kissed me softly, his full lips covering my mouth. He left a scent of Aqua Velva cologne all over my chest. "I'll call you tomorrow, babe."

"I love you," I said, but he never replied.

Climbing onto the bus, I put some coins into the hole and sat down to watch Max run back to the party.

Thirty minutes later I was home. Dad, as usual, was sitting in his recliner watching Johnny Carson in the living room. "How was the party?" he asked.

"It was fun." My voice sounded strange. I wanted to get to my bedroom before Dad figured out that I was high.

"I was starting to wonder if you were going make it home."

"Why wouldn't I make it home?" I didn't want to argue with him, but it was almost a habit by then.

"The buses stop running right about now."

"I'm home Dad, and I'm going to go to bed."

Diane was sleeping as I put on my pajamas and crawled under my sheets. Laying there I stared at the cottage-cheese ceiling. Patterns swirled and colors melted into each other. I wanted to be back at the party with Max. I wanted to share the psychedelic experience with him. I wanted to trip out on the ecstasy of teenage love, and it didn't matter where it took us. I just wanted to be with him.

*

It was Saturday night and Max and I were eating at the diner at Bay Shore Lanes. We were both high and were getting something to eat at the small family diner that was tucked inside. Earlier that day I had scored two rolls of red devils. Back then you could get four shiny bullet-shaped-capsules wrapped in foil for a dollar. I had made it clear to Max earlier that I was doling them out. We were sitting in a booth sharing fries and a burger, and catsup was dripping down Max's chin. I could tell he was feeling the effects of the two pills I had given him, as his voice was getting louder and customers were started to stare at us.

"Let's get out of here, Max."

"Where, yaw wanna go baby?" he said, his voice booming.

"Let's go for a walk."

We paid our bill and exited the double glass doors into the parking lot. We hadn't even crossed the street when Max started pressuring me for more pills. "Just give me one more baby," he said, slurring his words.

"No, Max. You're too fucked up already."

It was rare for me to hold any sort of limit, but I'd been with Max the week before when his face landed in a plate of spaghetti at Tommy's Diner. Thank God we were with friends who were able to help me get him home. But if he passed out now, I'd never be able to manage his dead weight. Max was an ex-jock and all lean, thick muscle. I loved everything about his body. His arms, chest, his perfect ass, until it was time to keep it upright. Then not so much. Besides, if he passed out it would draw exactly the wrong kind of attention for a girl trying to stay out of juvie.

As we stood next to a brick building, across from the bowling alley, Max was getting louder. "Just give me one," he said.

"Not now, Max."

"Come on! I can handle it." His jaw tightened; his dark brown eyes turned to slits.

"No," I said, stomping a foot.

I vaguely remember him slurring profanities, 'Shit, fuck, Fucking A,' before he spun around and punched his fist through a small window in the building.

"Max!" When I reached for his hand, blood gushed from his knuckle. He pulled out a blue bandana that he kept in the back pocket of his jeans and wrapped it around his hand. "See what you made me do?"

"I did that?"

"You won't give me any reds."

"Oh, geez Max." I reached into my pocket and relinquished the last two pills that were his. He threw them in his mouth and swallowed them dry. His tone changed instantly. "I'm sorry, baby," he said.

"Why did you do that?"

"I couldn't hit you because you're a girl." I would learn that this principal was deeply embedded in him.

"So, the window was better than hitting me?" I didn't understand his logic. Today, I can't fathom why we stood around discussing his behavior, but that's what we did. We had plenty of time to get the hell out of there, but since we didn't, eventually the police pulled up with red lights flashing. Two officers got out of their car.

"Oh hey, Max, what's going on buddy?" It's never a good sign when the cops know your boyfriend by his first name.

"Hey, Sarge." Max stood erect, his shoulders back. "Just talking to my girlfriend."

The officer assessed the area with his steely blue eyes. A broken window, a bloody hand wrapped in a bandana, it was easy to put the pieces of the scene together.

"What happened to your hand Max?" the officer said, his brow furrowed.

Max looked down. "I, ah, I..."

"Did you break that window, Max?"

"Well, I, ah, I, just... I sort of lost my temper and I..."

"Going to have to take you in then."

It all happened real quick after that. The officer pulled out his handcuffs and cuffed Max hands behind his back, before escorting him to the squad car, while the younger officer stayed with me.

"What's your name?" he said. "Where do you live?"

Completely sober by this point, I told him, and he wrote everything down in a small notebook. I was acutely aware of the two pills still in my front jean pocket.

"You need to pick your boyfriends more carefully, young lady," he said, with a pathetic nod to the car.

I looked over at Max, his chin deep in his chest.

"You got enough money to get home on the bus, Missy?"

"Yes, sir, I do."

"I want you to go straight home."

"Yes officer." I turned to leave.

While I didn't realize it then within the bubble of my privilege, I was probably given a lot of passes because of the color of my skin.

As I walked past the squad car, I mouthed to Max, "I will call your mom."

He nodded with a sad look on his face, looking like he had sobered up as well. But cops always have a way of ruining one's buzz like that.

As soon as I got home, I went to my bedroom to call Jenny, Max's mother, on my princess phone. I told her that Max had been arrested for breaking a window. She thanked me, and said she'd go down to the police station before hanging up.

The next day, Max called me saying he was cited out, but he was scheduled to appear in juvenile court for vandalism.

"You scared me, Max," I said, gripping the phone.

"I know, baby. I don't know what came over me."

There was a looming dark cloud that hovered over our relationship. The fear of Max being sent away was all I could think about. For a month Max and I became inseparable. One day I was in his bedroom lying by his side, while his mom was in the kitchen cooking, probably homemade tortillas and frijoles like she usually did. There was a black light, with walls painted black, inspired by one of Max's acid trips. I laid next to him in his twin bed with my ear against his hairless chest, listening to his heart. Hearing the pulsing thump inside his rib cage made me feel closer to any human being that I had in my entire life. We were talking about the possibilities of what could happen when he went to court.

"You won't get sent away." I beat back my fear with denial.

"The probation officer thinks I should go away somewhere."

"They won't do that to you."

He pulled me in a little closer with his strong arms. The illusion of protection had been my safety harbor, I couldn't bear the thought of being away from him.

A week later Max appeared in front of Judge Thomas, the same judge my dad and I had been in front of. I sat on one of the wooden seats that snapped and slapped the back of your thighs whenever you got up. I pulled down a baseball cap so the judge wouldn't recognize me. When it came time for Max to appear, there was a lot of legal jargon before Judge Thomas sentenced Max to a year in the Job Corps in Cottonwood, Idaho. The Job Corps was a government program that offered vocational training for teens and young adults. My heart felt like a vice grip was squeezing it inside my chest. Tears welled up in my eyes.

A week later I was standing with his entire family at the Greyhound bus station on 6th street. His mother, brother and two sisters were all there to see him off. Max set down his green duffle bag that was neatly packed.

"Write to me," he said.

"I will. I promise." Tears welled up in my eyes.

"Don't cry," He said. "I'll be back before you know it."

I looked down at my toes peeking out from flip flops.

"Wait for me," he said.

"I'll wait for eternity for you," I said, meeting his brown eyes. He kissed my mouth with his soft lips.

Max and I said I love yous before he said goodbye to his family. One of his sisters sobbed out loud, her chest heaving. Max's mother held onto her youngest son for the longest time. I was mesmerized by the deep bonds that ran within his family.

Max gave me one last anguished look, before climbing onto the bus. Tears streamed down my cheeks as he waved goodbye though the window. The air brakes released before the bus drove off.

After Max left, I spiraled into a deep hole of depression. Counting the days became an obsession for me. Eleven months and twelve days until he'd be back. Ten months and fourteen days. Friday became Monday, and back to Friday again. Time had become nothing more than a meaningless abstraction. Without him, life was unbearable, so once again, drugs became the answer. I started going to parties with girlfriends. I would often black out and not remember what had happened to me. The only things I had to look forward to were Max's letters.

One day one of those letters came, but this one was different. I went to my room and ripped it open, but when I started reading it, I realized Max had written me a Dear Jane letter. Apparently, someone had told him I was getting high and making a fool of myself at parties. He was breaking up with me. I was seventeen and wanted to die.

I thought it was the end of our relationship.

The Quake

After the break-up with Max, my life unraveled even more. I didn't care about staying out of trouble. I felt it was necessary for me to numb out the pain by getting high. Although I didn't recognize it at the time, it was fortunate my dad told my P.O or I might have ended up killing myself the way I was ingesting drugs. I was quickly sent back to Sylmar Juvenile Hall and when Mrs. Shelton came to visit me that time, she had some bad news to deliver in that white, windowless room.

"You're going to Youth Authority," she said.

"But that's for felons." My eighteenth birthday was just a week away, so I would be an adult soon.

"Look Wendy, we've tried hospitals, foster homes, drug programs and nothing has worked. You've given me no other choice."

My heart felt like it was plucked from my chest. I could barely breathe. I lowered down in the chair and crossed my arms over my chest. While turning eighteen might have meant more if I had been going to school or wasn't depending on my dad still to support me, I was still pissed off that my probation officer was controlling my life. All I wanted was for everyone to just leave me the fuck alone.

I turned 18 on February 5th, 1971 in juvenile hall. Obviously, there was no cake, no cards and no gifts from family or friends. I was alone, and there was nothing to celebrate–just the dreaded day I would be taken to Youth Authority to start my term.

Four days after my birthday and still in juvie, waiting to be taken to Y.A., I stared at my ceiling. I couldn't sleep. It was just after 6:00 AM when the mesh screen above me started to rattle like someone was banging on it from the outside. My initial thought was that it was some pervert-groundskeeper was trying to get my attention. I pulled the gray wool blanket over my head to hide. Suddenly the whole room shook, like a freight train was barreling underneath the ground. The room pounded and shook so hard I had to hold onto the sides of my bunk so I wouldn't be thrown off.

"Help me! Help me!" Someone screamed from down the hall.

We're all going to die. So, this is how it happens.

The room shook as the ground shifted. I had no idea what was going on. I thought it might be the end of the world. The door to my cell was locked. Quite literally nowhere to run. No way to run. I was trapped. Over the rumble I heard the officer yell from down the hall, "Everyone, get under your desks."

I pushed myself up and almost fell as I half crawled and positioned myself underneath the flimsy metal desk. I knew if the walls came down the desk wouldn't protect me but it was my only option. I hugged my knees into my chest as terror crawled up my spine. I wanted to scream for help, but I couldn't get enough air into my lungs. With each tense breath, I was on the verge of panic. My gaze darted around, searching the walls for any cracks that would indicate a complete collapse.

Ever since I was a kid with horrible night terrors, I had a deep-seated fear of being trapped, and there I was. Trapped. When the ground shook again, there was a sharp scream from the room next door.

Yep. I'm going to die in here alright.

Seconds or minutes went by. Time distorted. The earth began to settle. An eerie silence fell around like ash. Finally, I heard the sound of keys from further down the hallway, followed by the thud of locks being released. The officer was letting everyone out. From under the desk, I stretched my arm towards my sneakers and slipped them on. I was dressed in my blue gym shorts and a t-shirt that I liked to wear to bed.

I heard metal on metal and a thud before my door was unlocked. When I leaped up my legs were weak.

"Go outside to the field." The officer waved me down the hall.

The electricity had gone out, but I could still see directly in front of me. Halfway down the corridor there were two massive cracks splitting the cement wide open. Getting to the other side required that I jump onto a slender island of concrete. It looked far away and I was afraid I wouldn't be able to clear it, but I didn't have a choice. I took a deep breath before I leaped, but when my tennis shoe landed I slipped and one leg fell inside the crack causing the tibia of my right leg to hit the jagged concrete. My flesh tore open in two places just like the earth below me.

Fuck! Keep going before the earth shakes again.

Without any pain, I pushed myself up and out to the other side. When I looked down, blood was running down my leg. I had to keep moving as desperate girls were rushing behind and past me, trying to get out of the building.

Breathless, I made it outside. My body felt like I had run a marathon. Small groups huddled together across the field. It was an unusual sight: everyone gathered like that because the units were always kept separate to maintain crowd control. But there we were, with three or four correctional officers walking around trying to reassure us. Fear had become the great equalizer.

Then I saw Mariah, a statuesque seventeen-year-old who waved at me from the middle of the field, her blonde hair framing her face. Mariah was also on her way to Youth Authority, so we had recently become friends. I rushed over and threw my arms around her, forgetting all about the no contact rule.

"Are you alright?" she asked.

"I fell inside a hole." I showed her the blood on my leg.

"That doesn't look good at all." There was concern in her blue eyes.

"Have we been bombed? Are we being attacked?" Questions bubbled up from inside me.

"It's an earthquake."

"An earthquake." I suddenly understood.

For years I had heard about the San Andrea fault line. People were afraid when the big one hit, California would fall into the ocean. But I had never experienced a quake before, and to me what we experienced that day felt like the end of the world.

If the ground shook that hard in the Valley, I figured my home must have be completely gone because it was closer to the ocean than we were. "Oh my God. I hope my family is okay."

I had no idea that several miles away from me over 65 people had perished in the quake, crushed to death under a brand-new building at Olive View Medical Center. The Veterans Hospital buildings had also collapsed. I later learned that an entire freeway overpass had come down and would affect transportation for weeks to come. I also had no idea that the Van Dorman dam was close to breaching and that 80,000 people would have to be evacuated until the reservoir water went down. But even if I knew all of these facts, my main concern would still have been: What's going to happen me? With the earth shaking beneath my feet, adults were controlling my life.

*

We sat for hours on the grass field under a hot scorching sun. There were tremors followed by cries of terror. With the collective anxiety of us broken girls, panic attacks, hyperventilating and uncontrollable sobbing ensued.

One correctional officer felt so bad for us that she passed out cigarettes in an effort to calm us down. Like war buddies, there was a quiet bonding taking place. We had survived the worst event in our short lives together. It wasn't until late that afternoon when we were lined up and ushered to the parking lot where black and white county buses waited to take us to other detention centers in the Los Angeles area. After Mariah and I hugged goodbye, I walked through the diesel exhaust and pulled myself up the two steps to find a seat.

For the next half hour as we drove through the town of Sylmar it looked like a war zone. Train tracks twisted up like pretzels, entire store fronts crumbled, and houses destroyed. Leaning my forehead on the glass, I stared out the window. I could easily see the damage left by the quake, but there was no way of knowing that there was a fault line inside me that would end up destroying everything in my wake.

ADULT HOOD

Downward Spiral

After the quake, the two remaining Los Angeles Juvenile Halls were bursting at the seams. Girls were packed in like sardines, sleeping across the concrete floors. Apparently, probation officers were being pressured by the courts to let some of the kids go. I was one of those kids. By the beginning of March, I was back home and off probation for the first time in years.

Dad had recently gone bankrupt and moved into a pale-yellow house in an alley on the east side of Santa Monica. My brother Bruce lived in the converted garage, while Diane had moved out and no one knew where Jay lived anymore. The living room had hardwood floors, a couch and a tv in the corner. The round dining table sat outside a small kitchen that barely had enough room for one person to maneuver inside. It was certainly a downgrade from all the houses we lived before.

I had no idea what I was going to do now, but without a probation officer breathing down my neck and Dad not being able to tell me when to come home because I was legally an adult, I wanted to make up for lost time. Within weeks I was drinking with a vengeance and I'm not talking about the sugary, wine-spritzers I used to drink. I had graduated to Bacardi 151.

I had graduated to Bacardi 151 and would soon find myself detoxing at Rancho Los Amigos in Downey.

Then at nineteen I found myself detoxing at Rancho Los Amigo Hospital in Downey.

It was a brightly-lit open ward with partitions separating me from other patients who as far as I could tell, were mostly over forty. Nurses would come in with their crepe soles squeaking to take my vitals and check the I.V. that was dripping into my arm. The unit was filled with moans, groans and beeping sounds. I didn't think I belonged there.

Doctor Caplan came by to do a physical exam. He was tall, with long straight hair, his face stamped with a look of concern. He told me who he was, and had me lay on my back, his soft hands kneading my stomach. A frown passed over his face when the tips of his fingers dug under my right ribs. "Your liver is distended, Wendy," he said.

"What does that mean?"

"I think you might be an alcoholic."

I was highly insulted that he would say such a thing to me. In my mind alcoholics were the old men I saw lying in the gutter or the women who ended up living alone with fifty cats. Or even my Dad, but I was barely nineteen and just getting started.

"At this rate, you'll end up with cirrhosis by the time your thirty."

I didn't know what cirrhosis was, but I figured it wasn't a good thing. But honestly, I wasn't too concerned because I thought I'd probably never live to see twenty-one.

*

Shortly after the detox I went back home. I felt like I was walking on eggshells being around Dad. One day I was in the kitchen getting something to eat when he came up behind me and said, "You need to get a job, Wendy."

The hair on my arms bristled. "Get off my case."

"I've had to file for bankruptcy, and if it wasn't for Uncle Harold helping us out, we'd all be living on the streets."

Dad's threats of running out of money had been occurring for years, but I knew it was getting worse.

*

Instead of looking for work I made plans to hook up with a couple of girls whom I used to get loaded with. I don't remember everything about that night, but I do remember meeting them on the boardwalk. I remember taking a couple of red devils with them. I remember feeling a real good buzz. But pretty quickly, everything went dark. I don't remember getting stopped by the cops. I don't remember being put into a squad car. I have one blurry memory of being at a Santa Monica substation where the rude jailer said I was too loaded to stay in their facility. I remember being offended by his remark.

"Take her down to county," the jailer said.

I started to sober up when I was put in the back of the squad car. I remember pleading with the two cops, "Please let me go," slurring my words.

"Would you shut up?" The driver glared at me in his rearview mirror.

Apparently, cops weren't as easy to flip as my dad.

An hour later we were pulling into an enclosed parking lot with looped razor-wire running along the eight-foot wall. The car screeched to a stop. Both officers leapt out to retrieve me from the back seat. They probably wanted to get back to arresting real criminals. "I think you're going to like it here, Wendy," one officer said.

Leading me by the back of my arm, I flinched when there was a loud clang and the barred gate rolled open. Once we stepped forward into the small chamber, the gate closed with a loud bang behind us. So, this was it. This was the county jail. Where the grown-ups went.

The place was worse than any adolescent facility I had ever seen. The iron bars had layers of peeling green, brown and yellow paint. The walls were smudged with gray. There was a cold wind that blew through the tunnel-like corridors. Another gate opened to my left, and my two escorts handed the sheriff my paperwork saying something about a transfer. And then they were gone.

"Come with me, Missy," she said. I would soon learn that Missy was an endearment compared with the other terms the cops would use. Standing at a counter, she looked at the paperwork and said, "Possession of a controlled substance." This confirmed that the arresting officers had found the two remaining red devils on me. The officer pulled out a white band and clamped it around my wrist with a hole punch looking device. "This is your identification while here." It had my name and booking number typed on it.

I was ushered into a dingy holding tank with a bunch of women. Not teens anymore, but full-grown, angry-looking beaten down women. There were hookers, immigrants, old drunks, and derelicts. Their loud voices bounced off the walls of the cement room. It felt like I was being inducted into some bizarre, freakish circus side show.

At this point I was completely sober. Cops and jail have a way of doing that. Internally, I was freaking out, but I knew enough not to let it show. A gray cloud of smoke hovered just below the ceiling. The cement floor was littered with cigarette butts and partially eaten cheese sandwiches that they doled out to hungry inmates.

I made my way to a corner on the cement bench not making direct eye contact with anyone. I was usually pretty good at making myself invisible, but it's hard to disappear inside a packed holding tank. I felt someone staring at me. When I turned, a dark-haired woman, with penetrating blue eyes asked, "What ya in here for girl?"

"Drugs."

"How old are you?"

"Nineteen."

She shook her head. "Damn. I have a kid your age."

Where being older had given me clout in juvie, I felt vulnerable in county jail. I was a baby, a newcomer, a virgin to the system. There wasn't a buddy or a guide to walk me through the whole booking process. Just like everything else, I would have to do it alone.

After an hour of my mind eating itself alive, another fresh-faced officer with blond hair tied back in a small bun at the nape of her neck called me out. She wasn't much older than me and there she was upholding the law, while I was breaking it. At the time, I couldn't connect that it was our decisions that separated us and forged our paths. I blamed my fucked-up childhood for determining my fate.

Blondie's duties were to fingerprint me in a back room. Each finger rolled across ink pads and the prints were transferred onto index cards. Small lines taken from the tips of my fingers for the purpose of identification, that reveal the unique characteristics that could identify someone in the event of a crime. These were the days before computers and DNA, so it would be a few years before they would have a database that could immediately link your prints to a crime. But technology was moving along at a rapid speed, and one day my prints would identify me as I graduated to bigger crimes.

I was put in another cell for an hour or so, until it was time to go to a room with six shower stalls, plastic bins in front of each.

"Alright ladies, listen up. Your street clothes go in the bin."

The room was lit with an unremitting brightness. The floor was tiled with a drain in the center for hosing down the area. I glanced at the woman next to me. Her skin looked like parchment paper rippled by time. I stripped off my clothes and dropped them in the bin.

As I stood there naked, embarrassment rippled up my spine.

"You're going to wash your hair and pubic area with this solution," the officer said, giving us each a tiny Dixie cup of an amber solution.

"What's it for?" someone asked.

"In case any of you have bugs."

She turned a control on the wall and all the showers went on. "Get inside and wash up."

I stepped inside. A drizzle of lukewarm water streamed from the nozzle. At the very least I thought they could give us hot water. My teeth chattered uncontrollably. I wet my hair and reluctantly put the solution on my head. Some of it dripped down and burned my eyes.

"Hurry up ladies, we don't have all day."

A few seconds later the water went off. I still hadn't got all of the solution out. As I stepped out, my flesh was covered in goose bumps, my hair was a tangled mess. I leaned back when the officer got inches from my face giving me quick orders. "Run your fingers through your hair. Lift your arms. Open your mouth. Lift your tongue. Turn around. Pull your cheeks apart. Squat. Cough"

I could feel her gaze up my vagina. I felt like I was being inspected for quality control. I was nothing more than an animal to them. Nothing more than a piece of meat.

After that, we were issued a roll up with linens, a stiff towel, and a night shift inside. A county dress was given separately. The dresses were all color coded so the officers could track inmates. While a new admission dress was blue, for someone working in the laundry room it would be yellow. Afterward we were herded into another holding tank. By that time more of a somber mood that had fallen on the women inside. Maybe it was the eight hours of processing or maybe it was reality sinking in, but they were quiet.

I was finally taken to meet the on-duty nurse who was rushing around in a small exam room her with white shoes that squeaked. She was short and squat with her gray hair permed in tight curls. I thought she might want to know if I had some underlying medical conditions the county should know about, but that was not the case. "Take off your panties and get up on the table," she said.

"Why?"

"I need to give you a pelvic exam."

I couldn't believe it, but I was in no position to object. My life was not my own anymore. I was county property. I took my panties off and crawled onto the table covered in a thin tissue.

"Scoot down and put your feet in the stirrups." I did what she said, as her rough hands spread my knees apart and she reached over for some metal device, "This might be a little cold." She stuck it inside me. The speculum squeaked as it opened the walls of my vagina so she could peer inside. My body was not my own.

Thank God it was over quickly. And while I had no idea why that had been done, I would find out later they were trying to keep drugs from coming into the jail. Apparently, women were getting caught stuffing balloons of heroin inside their vagina. At the time, I thought I would never do anything like that, but saying "never" was like giving the universe the exact coordinates as to where I would later land.

When I got to the cell block the gate slammed behind me. A dim light illuminated a toilet and a metal sink in the corner. A woman was fast asleep, snoring on the lower bunk. Years of repression, sweat, and fear hung in the air like a toxic cloud.

It should have been no surprise to anyone that I ended up in a cell block in county jail, but I still wasn't ready for it. But then again, I wasn't ready for it when detective Morgan threw me in a cell for shooting off firecrackers when I was a teen. I wasn't ready when I was labeled incorrigible and sent to Sylmar Juvenile Hall and Camarillo State Hospital. I kept thinking one day my life would begin—a real life would begin. But there was always some obstacle in the way. Some unfinished business, some debt to be paid. And as I laid down on the skinny mattress, it was impossible to beat back the voices in my head that told me I was a loser and that I would never change.

Self-Supporting

Without having any previous adult rap sheet, I got out of jail the next day on an O.R. (own recognizance). A few weeks later I went to court and was placed on summary probation. Basically, the judge told me to get in school or get a job or else I'd find myself back in jail.

One day I went to visit my sister Diane in her two-story craftsman that she shared with three former classmates. Diane had a dark golden tan and her hair had been dyed blond. When we were living together our relationship had been strained, but at twenty and out on her own she was more big-sisterly than she had ever been before. She gave me a hug and said she was glad I was out.

"If it wasn't for that earthquake, I'd be in Youth Authority right now."

"So, the earthquake was a blessing." She smiled, revealing her perfect dimples that looked carved into her cheeks with an ice pick. "Let me show you around and then we can catch up."

A guy with a towel wrapped around his waist came out of the bathroom. "Excuse me ladies." He turned sideways to pass us in the narrow hallway.

In the kitchen, I whispered, "Who was that?"

"Some guy Emily brought home that hasn't left." She waved her hand in the air.

"He's really cute."

"They all are."

There was an old O'Keefe & Merritt stove, a breakfast nook and loads of dishes in the sink. "This is the kitchen, but I usually eat at work."

Diane told me she was working two jobs. One as a hostess at the Holiday Inn, and another as a waitress at Tiny Naylor's an all-night diner a few blocks away.

"Let's go to my room," she said. Her bedroom was decorated with posters of bands and photographs she'd taken in Hawaii on a recent trip. We sat down on the edge of her bed. "So how is it being home?" she asked in a serious tone.

"Dad wants me to get a job."

"What you need to do is get out of that house."

Diane had always said she was going to get as far away from the family as soon as she could, and she wanted me to do the same.

"But what am I supposed to do? I can't get a job. I don't have any skills."

I could see Diane's brain working behind her eyes. "I might be able to get you a job."

"Doing what?"

"Waitressing. We make good tips."

The following week, Diane got me an interview with the manager of Tiny Naylor's. I was surprised when he offered me the graveyard shift. Of course, I said yes. I was given two pumpkin-colored uniforms with white collars and told my hours would start at 11:00 PM each night – the same shift as Diane.

There was a learning curve, but I picked up on things quickly. I loved the feeling of having something useful to do even if it was setting tables and filling catsup bottles. I learned how to balance multiple plates up my arm without spilling any food. I learned how to get better tips by checking in on customers multiple times and how to flirt with a busboy or a cook so they'd have your back.

I soon discovered that the graveyard customers were different than daytime folks. Some of them shuffled in stinking of booze and cigarettes wanting to sober up. Others were theater goers who came in to dissect blockbuster movies with a friend. Some customers came in to fend off the loneliness of going home alone.

My absolute favorite group was a bunch of actors and actresses who came in after the clubs closed. As soon as they stepped in the door, you'd hear their laughter echoing throughout the L-shaped diner. They dressed like they had walked out of a scene from American Graffiti movie. The guys cuffed the bottom of their jeans while the girls were dressed in pedal-pushers, poodle-skirts, bobbysocks and Oxfords. Sometimes there were so many of them they took up two or three booths. Diane and I knew most of them by name.

I felt like these were my people. The artists, the misfits, the rebels. The ones that stood out in a crowd. But there was a part of me that was envious too, because they were going for their dreams, while I was too afraid to even try. Deep down I knew I would never use the acting lessons Gretchen had given me years before. The mere thought of being rejected in an audition terrified me.

One night around 2:00 AM Diane and I were retrieving the laminated menus from our favorite customers, when Diane started to pry. "So, what movies have you guys been in?"

The guy with slicked black hair, who went by the name Fonzie said, "Most of us just do background, but Paige here has done a bit of real acting."

"That's because I could sing a little." Paige had a black ponytail, short bangs and freckles splattered across her nose.

"I've heard you sing and it's more than just a little," I said.

The group were known for playing Name That Tune, a television game show where you'd hear a few lines of a chorus, and you'd have to try to guess the song.

"Well, let's see if y'all can name this tune." Closing her eyes, Paige sang with her raspy soulful voice that made everyone stop and look. I had heard the song many times in juvie. Everyone else had puzzled looks on their face, but when Paige was done, I blurted out, "Etta James, I'd Rather Go Blind."

"Wow! She got it right." Paige pointed at me with her bangles clanking up her arm.

"How do you know all these obscure songs?" Fonzie asked.

"Um. I listen to a lot of music." I shrugged.

"Wendy's been around." Diane nudged me in the ribs.

Diane had a big mouth and would often make the mistake of revealing things about me that I didn't want anyone else to know. I was constantly giving her instructions to not tell people that I had been locked up as a teen. But she always seemed to forget, the same way I would forget when she told me to ask her first if I wanted to borrow any of her clothes. That's just how it was growing up in our family, and I didn't know there was any other way.

Later, that night Diane and I were goofing around, and we came up with a plan to convince the cook to let us use his microphone that he called out orders on.

"Can we use your mic?" Diane asked.

"Por que?"

"To sing a song," Diane said.

"Bueno." He waved us behind the tall counter.

Outside, twilight chilled the air. Inside smoke swirled above our heads in the brightly lit diner. The gang of actors were probably on their tenth pot of coffee when Diane and I started singing Hit the Road Jack over the P.A. system. This time, it was the actors' heads that turned to watch the sister act. First there was a burst of laughter, but quickly they started to sing along. And while at times I secretly wanted to disappear, I also had the side of me that longed to perform. I'm living proof that one can live with both those conflicting desires for the rest of their god-damn lives if they so please.

Junkie

While I learned how to take orders and bus tables, I started to hang out with Chad who was a few years older than me. He was popular and non-threatening. Chad was an American Indian, six 6 foot 4 inches tall, with a long ponytail that hung clear down to the middle of his back. And he may have had a little crush on me, but I made it quite clear I wanted to be just friends.

One day Chad offered to pick me up after work. I welcomed the ride because it was better than taking the bus. When I crawled into his gray pickup truck, the seat was draped with a Navaho blanket that covered the fact that springs were poking through. On the floor were crumpled wrappers from McDonald's Big Macs and French fries.

"I made some pretty good tips today." I counted the dollars onto my lap.

"You feel like doing some heroin?"

I could tell he was serious. In the past I had been afraid of doing it but hearing girls talk in juvenile hall like it was the best thing ever, I wanted to try it for myself. "Sure," I said.

Chad turned toward me and lifted his tongue, revealing balled up balloons the size of marbles.

"Why do you have it in your mouth?"

"So, I can swallow the evidence if I get stopped by the cops." He winked.

"Wow! I would have never thought of that." I liked learning ways to get one over on the cops.

Twenty minutes later we were at a small hotel on Ocean Park Boulevard. I followed Chad's wide frame up the narrow pathway that had five rooms on each side. I was starting to second guess my decision, but not enough to make me change my mind. We entered Chad's motel room where he paid weekly. There were blackout curtains and a queen-size bed that took up almost the entire space. A television sat on top of a dresser at the foot of the bed and a two-burner hot plate and a tiny black fridge sat in one corner of the room.

"Have a seat." Chad nodded. Wasting no time, he spat the balloons into his hand. He had a big smile plastered on his face as he rolled them up and down against his pant leg. Chad had everything already set up on a small nightstand next to the bed. A syringe, a blackened spoon, a cup of water, cotton balls and matches.

He snapped the small knot of the balloon with his teeth and poured the contents into the spoon. Using the syringe, he sprayed water over the almond-colored powder. When it was saturated, he took the matchbook, folded it and ignited half the book. Black smoke spiraled upward as he held it under the spoon. "This is to get any impurities out of it," he said.

"It's not pure?"

"The dope starts off clean, but as it gets passed down the food-chain, dealers cut it so they can make more money. Sometimes they use baking soda, sometimes lactose, but sometimes they cut it with garbage that can make you sick."

I leaned over Chad's back and watched as the powder dissolved into a brownish-yellow color. The smell of Sulphur and burnt brown sugar filled the air. Seconds later, he balled up a tiny bit of cotton and plopped it in the spoon. He pulled half the liquid into the syringe, and then used a belt hanging on the doorknob to tie off his bicep. I cringed as he poked the syringe through the crux of his arm. I gazed at his face curiously as it seemed to soften as the dope went in. "Good shit," he said, pulling it out.

Chad pulled the remainder of liquid into the syringe and turned his attention toward me. I sat down on the edge of the bed still in my waitress uniform. "Your turn." My heart was racing as his dull eyes gazed at me.

As he tied off my bicep with the belt, Chad's forehead was beaded up with sweat. It was almost like I was watching a movie as I looked down at my arm, and the dull needle poked through my virgin vein. Blood gushed just before the amber liquid was pushed into my blood stream through that overused syringe.

Immediately, a soothing warmth spread out across my chest and flooded my brain. I closed my eyes as my chin drifted down to my chest. "Wow," was all I managed to say. Up until then, pills had worked okay, but I always seemed to get too sloppy on them. Getting blitzed on alcohol was good at a party or a club, but I hated the hangovers the next morning. I knew instantly that heroin was what I had been looking for all my life.

"You like it?" Chad asked.

"I do, I do, I really do... " I trailed off.

*

Using heroin in moderation proved to be challenging. It took all of the will power I could muster to curtail my shooting up to just my days off. Junkies would refer to this as chipping, but I was afraid my habit would get out of control.

I was fighting with Dad all the time and my life had no real meaning. I felt empty inside and had nothing to look forward to. So, when I went to visit Diane at her house, she made me a proposition that sounded enticing. "Want to go back-packing cross-country with me?" she asked.

Diane had already spent three months in Hawaii while working on her perpetual tan back when I was in juvenile hall. She wanted to hitchhike across the United States but didn't want to do it alone. I hadn't been anywhere because I had been too busy being an incorrigible teen, so an adventure sounded kind of fun. "But what about our jobs?" I asked.

"We can get a leave of absence or we'll get new jobs."

"I don't know, Diane." It was hard for me to make decisions.

"We'll stop drinking and you can lose the pounds you're always complaining about. And maybe you'll even quit smoking." She nodded to the cigarette between my fingers. And while Diane had suspected I was up to no good with Chad, she never said anything.

"That's not going to happen." I took a long drag.

The idea that I could stop using was enticing, but I just didn't know how to stop. I always felt consumed with cravings that surrounded me like my own personal weather system. Perhaps if I got away from my environment, got away from Dad, and got away from the memories of Max I could start living my best life. "Let's do it," I said.

For the next few months I had something to be excited for. We made plans to be gone for the entire summer. We would save three hundred dollars from our tips and purchase traveler's checks that we would keep in a secret money belt around our waist. We bought books like Planet Earth. We marked off our routes on the map. We bought essentials that we packed and repacked into our new backpacks.

One day while going through our supplies, Diane told me her friend, Randy wanted to go with us for the first two weeks in the Sierras.

"He's a great camper and he can show us the ropes," Diane said.

"Won't that be kind of weird?"

"Not at all." Diane shrugged.

The first time I met Randy he reminded me of a mountain man with his frizzy, unkempt red hair and a scruffy beard. He wasn't like the other guys I was used to, but then again, he didn't shoot up dope either. He was a nerdy Jewish boy who just happened to enjoy the outdoors.

"You girls are going to love being in the wilderness," Randy said.

"But what about bugs?" I asked, my biggest concern.

"Just bring some repellant and they won't even bother you." He batted his hand at my question like he was batting away a mosquito.

While he seemed thrilled to be taking two virgin-hikers into the mountains, I was a bit apprehensive of spending an entire two weeks in the mountains.

Road Trip

A week later I was loading my stuffed backpack into the back of Randy's van. Randy was dressed in a plaid shirt. He looked like he'd been living in the mountains all his life. When all the gear was packed, Diane hopped in the front seat. I got in the back.

"You guys ready for an adventure?" Randy revved the gas to amplify his excitement.

"We're ready," Diane said.

"We'll then, let's go." Randy shifted gears and pulled into the street.

On the drive Randy talked endlessly about fishing, camping, weather conditions. I daydreamed about other things. I wasn't sure what I wanted from the trip other than to lose some weight and stop doing drugs all the time. I figured a cross-country trip would be my own customized version of drug treatment; a way to remove myself from people who used and the triggers that kept me circling the drain. And maybe I'd get a whole new outlook on life.

The sidewalks and tall buildings disappeared and eventually the landscape turned into rectangular fields in various shades and textures of green, spreading out as far as the eye could see. I was puffing away, when Randy said, "You know the Surgeon General said cigarettes can be hazardous to your health."

Looking at the Marlboro scissored between my fingers, I said, "Get off my case, Randy." Tossing it out the window, I crossed my arms over my chest willing myself not to smoke for the rest of the drive.

Hours passed. The van laboriously climbed up a windy, narrow road. A patchwork of white clouds hung so low it felt like we could drive right through them. As we got higher the crowded trees began to block out sky. The luxurious smell of pine made all my senses awaken.

"Well, here we are kiddos." Randy made a sharp left into a dirt parking lot. I jumped out and lit up another cigarette while Randy opened up the back.

"Can't wait to catch us some trout," Randy said, holding his fishing pole in the air like a sword.

The plan was to hike into the Sierras for two weeks. Randy had mapped out the trail we were to take and knew roughly where we'd set up camp each night. He had warned us that the first part of the ascent might be a bit rough, but once we got that out of the way, he said, "The rest would be a piece of cake."

Standing at the back of the van, I laced my arms through the straps of my backpack. It was so heavy I was worried my knees might buckle from the weight. Diane and I had researched camping books for months to see what we should bring. In my pack: a flashlight, sleeping bag, pup tent, thermal underwear, parka, can opener, tuna, pinto beans, beef jerky and that was just the basics. It was recommended to carry a maximum of 40 pounds, and at one point I was ten pounds over and had to take some of my favorite clothes out. I pulled the waist strap, tightened the cinch and tried to stand erect. It was not easy by any standard.

"Let's head on out," Randy said, locking the van.

Gravel crunched beneath our hiking boots as Randy led the way. We soon found ourselves on a trail that zig-zagged up the side of the mountain. I had no knowl-edge of switchbacks back then and how strenuous they could be on the body. Within twenty minutes my thighs and calf muscles were burning. What had I been think-ing? I was 170 pounds and I was a smoker. I felt a stab of pain in my lungs. "I need to take a break," I said, gasping for air.

Randy and Diane stopped as I sat down on a boul-der, hands on knees.

"It's all those cigarettes you smoke," Randy said.

Not able to speak, I narrowed my eyes and gave him a hard look. We were barely into the first leg of our trip and Randy was starting to irritate me.

Ten minutes later we started to climb again. My back-pack felt like a sack of wet cement. It took two hours to arrive at our first campsite. My thighs were trembling like a nervous terrier as I slipped off my pack. Randy rushed around sweeping pines and stones away with his hiking boots. I sat down and listened to the sound of the gushing stream close by.

"Come on, sis, we need to set up our tents," Diane said.

Diane and I had gotten bright red pup tents. They were essentially plastic tubes. I pulled it out of my pack and tore off the original packaging. Once we found a place where Diane and I could be next to each other, I laced rope through the plastic, lashing it to two sturdy trees. I pulled it taut and used several fist-sized rocks to hold down the corners to make my triangle. I shoved my sleeping bag inside. I was doubting this measly hovel would be enough to protect me from the elements, let alone a wild animal.

An hour later, Diane and I were sitting in front of a crackling fire. Randy served us a pasty, brown stew concoction on tin plates. Although it tasted like cardboard, I was hungry, so I ate it. The sound of crickets and cicadas surrounded us in a high-pitch frequency. Randy regaled us with his knowledge of plant life, trees, using their proper Latin names. He knew what mountain the icy river runoff was coming from. None of it interested me.

"I'm going to hit the sack you guys." I pushed myself up. A flashlight provided me a thin strip of illumination that led me to my tent. I crawled inside and closed up the ends with clothing pins to keep the mosquitos out. I zipped myself into my cocoon of a sleeping bag. What I remember most about that first night was how hard the ground was and the fire burning in my legs. I tossed and turned through the night, my body aching in rebellious protest of the day's physical exertion.

Birdsong woke me up in the morning. As I stretched my legs out, every muscle ached, but all I wanted was a cigarette, so I lit one up and puffed in the privacy of my tent. I could hear someone moving around outside. I grabbed my fleece pullover and slipped it on. I unclipped the clothes pins and crawled outside. Slipping into my boots, I shuffled off behind a cluster of trees to pee. It was cold and the stream of steamy urine couldn't come out fast enough. Afterward I pulled my pants back up and headed to meet Diane and Randy at the fire.

"Have some coffee, Sunshine," Randy handed me a cup. "It'll wake you up. It looks like we got about ten miles before we'll hit our next campsite," he announced.

"Ten miles? You've got to be kidding," Diane said.

"Don't be such a sissy," Randy said.

"When will I be able to work on my tan?" Diane was always trying to maintain a sun-kissed look.

"You'll be able to get some sun once we get there," he said.

Diane rolled her eyes as I grabbed my nearby backpack.

"I think I packed too much stuff." I peeked inside. "I think I need to get rid of some things."

"Me too." Diane nodded. The mouths of our packs gaped as we reached inside and started unloading.

"I don't need all this food," I said, holding up a can of beans.

"But what will we do with it?" Diane asked.

"I'm going to leave it here for the next hungry hiker that comes along."

A half hour later we were on the trail again. My legs throbbed. Annoying flies buzzed around my face. Sweat dripped down my back. My pack still felt too heavy. "Hold up you guys," I said, out of breath. "I need to get rid of more stuff."

"Can't you wait till our next stop?" Randy asked.

"No! It's breaking my back." I sat on a boulder and abandoned cans of tuna and one of the books I had brought. When Randy went off to pee, I turned to Diane and whispered, "This is fucking brutal."

"I know. I know."

"Can't we go back?"

"Randy would be so pissed off. He has been planning this trip for months."

"This is not fun."

We somehow made it to our next campsite and set up camp. The following day Diane and I tried laying on a massive boulder in our bathing suits to tan while Randy was off fishing. The flies wouldn't leave us alone. "Fuck! I can't do this."

"I'll just have to tell Randy we're not cut out for this camping shit," Diane said.

When Diane told Randy, he was livid. He didn't say a word as we marched back down the mountain. The tension was palpable as he loaded up the van.

"Sorry Randy it didn't work out," I said.

Silence.

Later, when Randy dropped us off on the side of the road for the next leg of our trip, hitchhiking to Scottsdale, Arizona. Diane and I both waved and smiled as he took off. Randy did not wave back.

Taos

As soon as our thumbs went out, we got a ride from two, long-distance, trucker drivers in a semi-truck. What I remember most about that ride, was how they kept themselves awake by spooning 'mini-bennies' into their mouths and chasing it down with hot coffee. They talked so much I was relieved when we got another ride all the way to our destination.

Taos, New Mexico is situated east of the Rio Grande and south of the Sangre de Cristo Mountains--the Blood of Christ, in Spanish. It seemed a fitting name as there was something sacred about the land. It had an energy that resonated deep within my cells. Our last ride dropped us off near the middle of town. Excitement rippled through me as the air was soaked with so much possibility. "Let's go look at the jewelry," I said.

Diane and I strolled through town with our backpacks towering behind our heads. The heat of the sun caused sweat to drip down the narrow of my back. We passed by art galleries, coffee shops, and Native Americans sitting with their trinkets on bright woven blankets. A woman with almond skin and sleek blue-black hair sat in front of hand-crafted jewelry. When I leaned over the weight of my pack almost toppled me over, but I was able to kneel and catch myself. I wanted a souvenir that was light, so I picked up a pair of dangling silver earrings that caught my eye. "Look at these." I held them up for Diane.

"Pretty damn cute."

Turning back to the woman. "How much?" I asked.

She held up both hands showing me her calloused palms. I paid her the ten dollars and tucked the earrings into my front pocket. We continued to walk until we came to a small taco stand. I got a fat burrito and Diane ordered tacos. We sat on the grass in the central courtyard to chow down. I was just stuffing the last of it into my mouth when a couple of guys walked up. One had a cowboy hat, shoulder-length hair and a patch covering one eye. The other was short and stalky with light brown hair.

"Howdy, girls," Eye Patch said.

"Oh hey," I replied.

"Where you girls from?" he asked.

"Los Angeles," Diane said

"What part?"

"Santa Monica," I said.

"Oh wow! I lived in the Valley for a while."

I still wasn't a big fan of the Valley, but when you're on the road for some reason, geography can bond you instantly with a stranger.

"You mind if we join you?"

"Sure. Have a seat," Diane said.

We chatted it up with our new friends, Dave and eye-patch, Rick. They told us how Taos provided a simpler lifestyle than we were used to in big city life.

"Where are you girls staying?" Rick asked.

"Not sure yet," Diane said.

"I know of a beautiful place by the river if you girls are looking to camp out."

The back packs made us look like campers, but I would have certainly been open to a five-star hotel.

"How far is it?" I asked.

"Just outside of town. I can show you if you like?"

That was it, and within minutes we were loading our backpacks into Rick's battered pick-up truck. We all squeezed in the front seat, shoulder against shoulder. Then Rick asked the one question that everyone asked at the time, "You girls like to get high?"

My ears perked up. While the plan was to clean up our acts, I was finding sober traveling a bore. "Yes," I replied.

"Wendy, we're supposed to stop." Diane said.

"It's okay to get high once in a while," I said.

When I looked into her eyes, they bore into mine. Diane was a good Catholic girl compared to me, but the fact there were now three of us in favor, she couldn't help but succumbed to the peer pressure. "I guess one time wouldn't hurt." She shrugged.

"Have you ever tried heroin?" Rick looked back and forth to each of us to gauge our reactions.

There was a pause.

"Just once," Diane said.

"Why? Do you have some?" I asked.

"I can get Mexican tar right down the road," Rick said.

Maybe I talked Diane into it. Maybe we were just ready for a different experience. Maybe we were out of our element, but somehow the decision was made to score heroin, and lucky us, we'd be the ones paying for it. As we drove just outside of town, Rick pulled over in front of what looked like a thrift store. "We'll be right back girls," Rick said.

After the guys slipped into the dilapidated house, I gazed at the baby strollers, bikes, pans, chipped plates and candle holders that sat out on rickety wooden table out in front. Two thick watchdogs strained against chains as they barked just off to the side.

"Are you sure you want to do this?" Diane asked.

"We're on an adventure, right?"

"But we don't even know these guys."

"They seem alright to me."

A few minutes later the guys came back. When Rick smiled, I noticed he had a tooth missing. The hole looked like a blacked-out window of an abandoned building. "Well ladies, were in business." He held out his palm with a small triangle of folded paper.

My face and ears grew hot with anticipation. It was a feeling I got whenever I was about to do heroin. Rick started the truck and within minutes we were driving further away from town, passing chaparral, strange rock formations and Ponderosa pine that reached toward the sky. We turned off the main road and the ground became bumpy as we pulled up along the river's edge right next to a lush green meadow.

"This is it," David announced.

"It's gorgeous." Diane and I were impressed.

As we got out of the truck the ground crunched beneath our feet. The air smelled of fresh pine. The river bubbled over rocks as it rushed down stream. That's when the syringe came out. "We have to shoot up?" Diane said, her brow creased.

"Mexican tar is way too thick to snort," Rick said, emptying the black gummy substance into a spoon. David got an old McDonalds soda cup from the floorboard of the truck and retrieved a bit of water from the stream. After putting a little water in the spoon, Rick held matches underneath while Dave with his eyes bugging out leaned forward.

"I'll go first." I raised my hand. After all, it was our money and I wasn't about to be shy.

"I think you're going to like this kiddo." I watched as Rick poked the needle through my skin causing the blood to rush into my vein. A warmth spread out across my chest and I felt the familiar opiate embrace throughout my body. The instant that needle slid out I rushed over to the bushes to throw up the burrito I had eaten just an hour before.

"Are you alright?" Diane asked.

"Yeah, yeah. I'm fine." I said, gasping for air.

I don't remember much after that, but as it turned out Diane was not a fan of throwing up under a blanket of stars with strange guys. And unlike me, she would never do heroin again.

Saved by the Bus

First thing the next morning we ditched the guys. Our plan was to head north to Denver. We figured if we got rides fast enough, we could be there in five hours. We hadn't even been out there ten minutes when Diane started to complain. "No one is picking us up," she said.

"But we barely started."

One of her hiking boots came down hard. "I want to go home."

My cheeks turn hot. I could not believe she was pulling this shit. "But, but why?"

"Shooting up heroin with a couple of losers is not my idea of a good time."

"We can't just give up." The last thing I wanted to do was go back home with Dad.

"I don't care. I want to go home," she said, her mind seemingly made up.

"But, Diane..." I trailed off just as a yellow school bus pulled over to the side of the road and its accordion door flew open. "Where you girls headed?" the driver asked.

I looked at Diane and back at the driver. "Ah, we were headed to Colorado. I think."

"Well you're in luck, ladies. We're going that way, so hop on in." He pushed back his black oily bangs away from his face.

"Diane?"

Biting her lip, she said, "Alright. Alright."

Pulling myself up the two steps, I was instantly hit with the smell of stale beer, tobacco and sweat. In the back were four mattresses with a hippie couple sitting on one of them. A blond girl with beads waved enthusiastically. I smiled back at her.

"My name is Cornelius and that's Billy," the driver said.

Billy was sitting shotgun. He was black with a colorful tie wrapped around his forehead and a thin mustache. He reminded me of Jimi Hendrix. "Welcome ladies," he said.

"That's Fred and Sally back there." Cornelius skin was scarred with acne and he had a slight overbite that flared his lower lip out. "We're headed to the Rainbow Festival."

"What's that?" Diane leaned in closer to Cornelius to hear.

"An annual 4th of July event. People come from all over the country to hang out and listen to music."

"Wow! That sounds far out," Diane said.

"You're welcome to join us if you like. I only ask you chip in for gas."

"Let's go Diane!" I figured this was more of the vacation she had been looking for.

I could see her mind working behind her eyes. "Okay. Let's do it."

"Groovy! Feel free to make yourself at home," Cornelius said.

Shifting gears, Cornelius stepped on the gas. I grabbed the bar to keep from falling. When the bus rolled onto the highway, I nearly lost my balance. The front of the bus had two rows of seats. The back had four mattresses lined up side-by-side with a slender aisle down the middle. Fred wore a beige poncho and his girlfriend, the beaded Sally, sat shoulder to shoulder on one of the mattresses. Diane and I plopped down across from them.

"Where ya guys from?" Diane asked.

"Tampa, Florida," Fred said. "Where you girls from?"

"Santa Monica," Diane said.

"Billy and I are from Venice," Cornelius yelled over his shoulder.

It turned out we had several friends in common. This put us at ease with Cornelius and Billy right away, because somehow, we were linked by place. Fred lit up a joint and took a long-drawn-out inhale. When he passed it to me, I turned it down because I didn't want paranoia to creep in.

We drove through miles of mesquite and cacti, until the Sangre de Cristo with its aspen-covered mountainsides came into view. Diane and I pushed ourselves up on our knees to peer out the smudged, hazy window. Fruit stands streaked by. Adobe homes in front of land that seemed to go on forever. Every time the bus took a turn I would lean into Diane or she would lean into me. The swaying back and forth made my eyelids heavy.

"I'm just going to close my eyes for a bit," I said, laying down on the Navajo blanket covering the mattress. I rested my head on my extended arm and drifted off.

I don't know how much time passed but when I woke up, we were pulling into a parking lot. I rubbed the sleep from my eyes and moved up front where Diane was sitting shotgun. "What are we doing?" I asked.

"Getting some supplies at the market," Diane said.

Once we parked, we all exited the bus. I had to squint back the late afternoon sun. I couldn't help but notice people staring at us as they walked by. One woman had a snarl on her pinched round face as she passed by. She was probably thinking we were nothing but a bunch of anti-war hippies, and therefore we were nothing but trouble.

Turning back to my bus-buddies, I asked, "What town are we in?"

"Pueblo, Colorado" Cornelius said.

"We need to get something to eat," Diane said.

I followed Diane into the store. Once inside we grabbed an assortment of fruit, chips and sodas. "What about getting some wine?" I asked. It wasn't hard for us to forget all about our plans to quit drinking or at the very least, to cut down. Moments later we were studying the bottles of booze in the alcohol aisle.

"You think this is enough for everyone on the bus?" Diane held up a fifth of cheap wine.

"Better get two," I said. Diane tucked another bottle under her arm.

Once in the check-out line, I discreetly pulled out one of my traveler's checks that were hidden in a money pouch belted around my waist. Diane and I had each brought $350.00, figuring we could live off a $100.00

a month. I don't remember how we came up with that amount, but we thought it would be enough.

Bags in tow, Cornelius was already behind the wheel of the bus. "Whatcha got girls?"

"Some wine." Diane gave a dimpled smiled.

As we drove past the Rockies passing the bottle of wine around there was laughter and sharing of stories with one other. Somehow the decision was made to by-pass Denver and go to Wyoming with our new friends. While a lot of the drive remains a blur, I do remember feeling relieved that Diane wasn't complaining, and there was no more talk about going home.

Rainbows

I was sleeping in the back of the bus when voices woke me. My tongue felt like a shriveled prune. My head throbbed. I was hungover from all the wine from the day before. My plan to cut back on drinking wasn't working. I couldn't seem to get through one day without sending some sort of mind-altering substance through my veins. I made excuses by telling myself it was a vacation, and how else was I supposed to have a good time? But each time I drank I would later be consumed with regret.

I threw back my sleeping bag and went up front towards Billy, Diane and Cornelius. Fred and Sally had stayed in Boulder with some friends, so it was just the four of us now. I sat down next to Billy and gazed out the window at the caravan of cars and the half-naked hippies carrying supplies down a dirt road. Some were barefoot, some wore sandals, and others had on tennis shoes, but all of them wore smiles. "This is it?" I cupped a hand over my mouth to guard everyone from my morning breath. Billy nodded.

"Ready for the most epic gathering of your life ladies?" Cornelius said.

The thought of interacting with so many people made me anxious. My foot tapped against the aisle of the bus. Billy pulled a soft pack of smokes from his pocket.

"Cigarette?"

"Thanks Billy." I lit up and took a long drag.

Billy was a mellow saxophone player. I never appreciated the sax until I heard him play it on the bus. I remember the soft notes that he coaxed from the instrument soothed me from the inside out. In my mind, Billy was the coolest cat that ever walked the planet.

"Almost everyone is naked here," I said, gazing past him out the window.

"Cool. Right?"

To someone else I might have come off as a free spirit, but I wasn't really a hippie. I figured hippies weren't ashamed of their bodies and I most definitely was. They believed in free love. I had no idea what real love actually felt like. In the sixties the hippie movement had been world-famous for being willing to engage in protests for world peace. World peace? I couldn't even get my own thoughts in my own head to coexist in harmony.

I thought the hippie mythology dictated that they'd engage in random sex with as many people as they possibly could. It wasn't the sex that bothered me—it was just that I hated every part of my body. Undressing in front of strangers was a type of vulnerability that was beyond my reach. The swells, the curves, the thickness of it all. It felt like too much baggage stuffed inside one suitcase. Besides, by then I'd learned sex was overrated. It was something guys did when they wanted quick gratification. I had to be drunk or high to give my body away.

"I'm going to park here, and we can walk the rest of the way." Cornelius pulled over and the bus tilted sideways onto the soft shoulder of the road. "We'll be here for a few days so take what ya need. Don't worry about food, they have plenty."

Diane and I went to the back to get situated with our backpacks. I wasn't going to make the same mistake as we did in the Sierra's and bring too much stuff. "What are we going to do? Everyone here is naked," I whispered.

"I'm not taking off my clothes," she whispered back.

At the core Diane and I were just a couple of prudish Catholic girls. We exited the bus, me in my tennis shoes, a halter top and jeans, Diane in cutoffs.

The grassy prairie land spread out on all sides, bordered by blue majestic mountains in the distance. The landscape seemed carefully designed by an artist who had sketched a vibrant painting with patterns of fine, subtle strokes. A fleshy girl with grapefruit-sized boobs said, "Welcome to paradise, family."

A man with dreadlocks as thick as ropes running down his back was pushing his girlfriend in a red wheelbarrow. A shirtless skinny guy had a guitar strapped on his back, but his whole face lit up when he smiled. The sun was dazzling bright, casting tall shadows behind everyone that walked by. The pounding of drums could be heard coming from down the road.

"Far fucking out," Cornelius said.

The Rainbow Family is a counter-culture group that to this day put on yearly camping events known as Rainbow Gatherings. These Gatherings have always been non-commercial, with the focus being on World Peace through prayer, meditation, visioning, drum circles and music. Their philosophy is creating intentional community through spirituality in order to invoke conscious evolution. The events are open to all people from all walks of life and beliefs. The organization has no leaders and its stated goal is to achieve peace and love on earth. But what was really special about the gathering of 1973, is that attendance was over 20,000.

That year, the festival was being held on the Wind River Reservation, the seventh largest reservation in the country at 2.2 million acres. The Rainbow Family members had been collaborating with the elders of the Shoshone tribe for months. They had promised that the land would be just as pristine as when they got there. Anything brought in would be taken out, and unlike at Woodstock, the Rainbow family had a reputation for staying true to its conservationist word.

We followed the colorful arrows posted on trees. Once we passed a whimsical "Welcome" sign we entered a meadow of brilliant green grass under a sheet of blue sky. We passed a large circular gathering spot, then a childcare center and a first aid station. I was struck by how organized everything was. It was not at all what I had expected.

The kitchen had a long grill with several cooks already preparing dinner in massive steel pots. There was a handmade mud oven with a woman in a flowy skirt kneading dough for homemade bread. Tables and chairs were setup under tie-dyed sheets where people gathered to talk or hang out.

We helped ourselves to coffee until we decided to stake a claim on a piece of real estate for camp. Diane and I set up our pup tents, while the guys would sleep on the ground underneath the stars.

"Let's go explore," Diane said. Off we went.

Everything was green, with bursts of wildflowers. A group of children was laughing and splashing around in the creek. People strolled by us on the path smiling and greeting us with, "Hello, sisters" or "Hello, family." I was really touched by this outpouring of strangers' love that was so unlike my life back home.

Following a trail by the creek, we came to a plastic teepee with steam seeping from the top. A man crawled out a small opening at the bottom and dove into the nearby creek. He was completely naked. Then a girl with a long body, lithe as a crane, did the same. Feeling like we were standing out more keeping our clothes on, Diane suggested we take off just our tops. I wanted to fit in, so that's all it took. In no time we were stripping down and crawling inside the makeshift sauna. There were others in there, but it was dark and all you could see were silhouettes. Steam drifted off a pile of rocks in the center. My flesh started to bead with sweat. The built-up grime that had become like a second skin started running from my body, dripping onto the ground. The scalding air filled my lungs until they felt like they might explode. Finally, I crawled out the slit and jumped into the icy cold creek. The sudden shift in temperatures sent shivers through me.

That night we sat in an orchard under a sapphire moon with millions of stars lighting up the sky. A joint and a jug of wine were passed around. Folk singers strummed acoustic guitars. A juggler tossed oranges in perfect arcs in the air. Groups camped next to small fires, faces illuminated by burning embers. People were hugging and stroking each other with genuine tenderness. It was a demonstration of worship of unity and love. The sound of laughter filled the warm summer air. It was incredible how a kid who had been in and out of institutions for years ended up in a scene like that. I was blown away.

*

The next morning was the 4th of July. Everyone was to remain silent till noon in order to contemplate world peace. In the early seventies, after years of protests, draft-dodging, and riots in the streets it seemed we were nearing the end of the Vietnam war. The Rainbow Family believed that envisioning a peaceful world in the mind could actually invoke change in the outer world. Having spent years caught up in the juvenile justice system, it all seemed a bit like magical thinking to me. But as they say--when in Rome.

The silence turned out to be harder than I could have imagined. My thoughts continued to buzz around my brain like bees in a jar. Eventually, I wandered off by myself until I came to the edge of a sweeping field of rust-colored grass. I gazed out at the field as a soft breeze soared over the tips of the tall stalks. The colors shifted from light to dark shades of golden, earthy brown. And then back again. I lost track of time, taken in by the movement of the grass. My brain quieted.

I started to feel a deep connection to nature, and although I didn't quite realize at the time, I had gotten a glimpse of peace.

Later, back at the sacred circle, a parade of children, tailed by adults marched in at noon, holding a colorful ribbon over their heads. Everyone gathered around the hand-made, stage as an older Shoshone Indian in full indigenous attire chanted a prayer for world peace. When he finished, we all chanted "ohm" from deep in our chests, a sound that reverberated through the crowd like a wave.

All of a sudden, the celebration sprung into full gear. Congo drums erupted in a tribal beat. Girls danced in bare feet on the grass, arms spiraling towards the sky. Diane and I joined in. We couldn't help it. It was magical. When I look back, I didn't realize at the time the power of community, silence and nature could have on one person. It would take years before those same principals the Rainbow Family were promoting would become central elements to me getting sober later on.

*

At some point during the Rainbow festival Diane and I had contracted dysentery. We were on the road on our way to Colorado for just a few hours when it hit me. It felt like some invisible force was gripping my intestines.

"Cornelius, we need to stop at a bathroom," I said, panic rising in my voice.

"What's wrong?" he asked.

"I have to go to the bathroom. Now!"

A minute later Diane chimed in. "Me too. Hurry Cornelius, or else I'm going to shit in my pants."

Cornelius pulled over at a one-stop gas station that had food, bathrooms and a large parking lot. "Here you go." he opened the door.

Diane and I rushed off the bus and into the station, grabbing two of the stalls in the bathroom. There was a gush of liquid that echoed off the stark walls. Instantly, my stomach coiled ready to spurt again. Diane and I insisted that we couldn't leave the station. We needed to be in close proximity to a bathroom at all times.

The guys surprised us by bringing us wet towels for our foreheads while we squirmed in the back of the bus. It wasn't until the next day that we were able to get back on the road again. For two days we stopped at gas stations using their bathrooms. We might have gotten the dysentery from all those free-spirited hippies washing their bodies in the creek. We might have gotten it from the drinking water or eating bad fruit. But by the time the symptoms subsided, I was rung-out, but thrilled at the fact that I had dropped twenty pounds.

Central City

Nestled in the mountains just west of Denver is an old mining town called Central City. Founded in 1859 during the Gold Rush, the town was originally known as one of the richest square miles on earth. In its heyday the town boasted an opera house, gambling halls, saloons and brothels, but by the early 70s the economy had turned the gold into a flood of tourists.

Because of its riches, the town flourished. Several opera houses sprung up, and The Central City Opera House still holds performances today.

We landed there through Jack, a rugged bearded fellow we'd met at the Rainbow Festival. He was going to visit his friend Sarah and invited us to come along. As the bus pulled onto Main Street, Diane and I kneeled on the mattress to get a better look.

"Here we are, girls," Jack said.

"Ahhh...this place is so cute," Diane said.

After parking Billy, Cornelius, Jack, Diane and I stepped out onto the cobblestone street.

"Let's go say hello to Sarah," Jack said.

We followed Jack, clopping down the wooden-planked-sidewalks to the local saloon. It was mid-afternoon and Sarah was tending bar and taking orders at the same time. She was immediately friendly and greeted us all with hugs and then led us to a high-backed wooden booth in the corner. What I remember most about her was her muscular arms and thick brown hair.

After serving us burgers and fries she joined us in the booth. It was mostly small talk. The requisite questions: "Where you guys from?" "How long you been on the road? "What's it like living on a bus?" But the conversation eventually drifted to where we were going to stay. We explained to her how there were enough mattresses on the bus for all of us to sleep.

With that same smiling openness, Sarah offered for the girls to spend the night at her spot.

Diane and I looked at each other. "It might be nice to get a break," Diane said.

Sleeping bags tucked under our arms, we followed Sarah down a dirt road with tiny rocks that led out of town. The farther we got the more spread out the neighborhood became. Unnamed dirt roads splintered off in different directions. At one point we passed a graveyard with headstones spread out across a green patch of lawn.

"A lot of miners died here in the 1800s and early 1900s," Sarah said. "Men will crush through two tons of rock to find a single ounce of gold and consider themselves to be lucky. One day it's all going to catch up to us...but by then, it'll probably be too late."

Geometric fields each with a different texture spread out as we entered a low-lying valley. We passed a gushing creek that came down from surrounding mountains, with young pine trees sprouting up all around it. While some of the land was green there were patches of brown caused by heavy machinery and years of mining. A stony precipice came into view where an old mine was carved into the side of the mountain, and the rim of a huge pit. All of the sudden I heard the familiar clip-clops of horse's hooves coming up from behind. A cowboy with perfectly trimmed sideburns appeared atop his steed, towering above us. He tipped the brim of his hat as he trotted by.

"Howdy, Roy," Sarah said.

"Cowboys live out here?" I asked.

"More like ex-bikers who are running from the law or want to get off the grid."

Growing up, I watched shows like Bonanza and Rawhide, fantasizing about living in the Wild West. I always had a special place in my heart for outlaws and Indians, which we still called them at the time. They were the rebels, the underdogs and the outcasts. I related to them, in my backwards juvenile delinquent kind of way. As Cowboy Roy became nothing more than a cloud of dust, I thought back to when I rode horses at Crestwood Stables. I missed the feeling of being on the back of a galloping horse my hair whipped in the wind and my thighs gripped to stay on its muscular back. I started thinking that maybe Central City might be a good place for me to settled down and live. A place I could finally call my home.

"This is it," Sarah said.

The cabin was rustic, with a rotting deck and a swooping roof that looked like a baseball cap pulled down over the porch. A single rickety rocking chair sat to one side. Clay pots with yellow daisies were lined up under a small window with shutters. Shovels, hoes and other gardening tools leaned against a wall.

Sarah opened the door, which creaked like an old woman, and revealed a black pot belly stove sitting in the corner. Several tall kerosene lamps were ready for when the sun went down.

"You'll have to sleep on the floor," Sarah said. "I only have one small bed in the other room."

Later that night we drank wine and shared stories. It was nice to be able to talk without the guys around for a change. At one point, Sarah's eyes filled with tears as she told us about her boyfriend leaving her just months before. "He didn't like the winter here," she said. "Without electricity or running water it can get brutal sometimes, but he knew that before signing up."

My thoughts drifted back to Max, whom I hadn't spoken to for years. I heard he had enlisted in the Army and was stationed somewhere in Germany. I figured he never thought about me anymore.

The three of us talked into the early morning hours. Eventually my eyes drooped to half-mast and I crawled into my sleeping bag, falling asleep in the corner.

I woke up with a strong urge to urinate. Diane was curled up in her sleeping bag a few feet away. I pulled on my boots. The floor creaked as I tip-toed out the door. The air was crisp as I made my way to outhouse down a dirt path. The cubicle reeked with the smell of shit and urine. I held my breath, wondering how Sarah got the sewage to a chemical plant.

When I got back, Sarah came out of her small bed-room with a bulky down coat and Diane was awake now.

"Can you gals go fetch some water?"

I barely made my bed when I was home, but I agreed.

"Of course," Diane said, pulling on her boots.

Sarah handed us each a bucket.

"How does anyone survive this place?" Diane said, as we walked down the road.

At the creek we filled the buckets with murky water. Mosquitos landed on the water with weightless legs. Larva scurried just under the surface. Mossy rocks sat on the bottom.

"This isn't fit for human consumption," Diane said.

"The miners did it, so I'm sure it's okay."

"Yeah. And all the miners are six feet under now. Might have been the water that killed them."

Back at the cabin, Sarah grabbed the bucket with her stubby fingers, pouring water into a pot and placing it on the pot belly stove. After it came to a boil, Sarah poured it through the filter into a silver coffee pot.

For the next few days we hiked the nearby trails or got joyfully drunk in the town bar.

After the sun went down, the guys would come up and we'd all sit on the front porch. Boots clomped across the deck as Sarah passed everyone a can of beer. Cornelius cradled his treasured Gibson guitar in his arms. A sax laid across Billy's lap. Two neighbors' dogs wrestled playfully in the dirt nearby.

"What are you going to play?" Sarah asked, sitting down in her rocker.

"Any special requests?" Billy asked.

"Something mellow," she replied.

"Can you play 'Heart of Gold'?" Diane said, pressing the palms of her hands together.

Cornelius set his beer down and began to strum his guitar with his long hair falling in his face. Then Billy started in on the sax with the sound echoing throughout the valley. Sarah sang harmony with her ethereal-angel voice. Midway through the song, Jack, put his harmonica to his mouth, making a shaking vibrato sound as he jerked his head. Within minutes neighbors from nearby cabins joined us. I sank into those moments, with faces partially illuminated by kerosene lamps. The sky became large. Cowboys in a dusty little town, the twang of a guitar chord could do me in. I could have stayed in the hills of Central City forever, but eventually adventure called, and we hit the road.

Chi Town

Billy had gone home, so it was just Cornelius, Diane and myself rolling into Chicago. The city was vibrating with a frenetic energy. A rattling urban sprawl of brick, asphalt and overhead trains. With its history of Al Capone, gangland violence and bootlegged liquor, Chicago intrigued a girl who'd done time in juvenile hall. I squinted at the bars, the eateries, and the liquor stores as they zipped by with splashes of graffiti scribbled haphazardly on the walls. The littered sidewalks looked like they belonged to the pimps and drug dealers.

"It looks filthy here," Diane said. "We should just keep on going."

There was a grind of metal as Cornelius shifted gears and stepped on the clutch. "We just got here. Wait till you see the rest of the city."

Minutes later we turned onto Lake Shore Drive and it was totally a different scene. One side of the highway featured a skyline punctuated with a wall of towering skyscrapers. On the other side, Lake Michigan, flanked by parks and slivers of beach where people walked their dainty pedigree pups. The sidewalks were smooth and clean. This was obviously a neighborhood for the upper class. Chicago, a city well-defined by the haves and the have-nots.

There was a sputter from the engine. I grabbed the metal bar in front of me, to brace myself. It didn't sound good.

"Oh shit!" Cornelius said.

The bus had been breaking down all the way across the country. It needed repairs in Colorado, in St. Louis and in Oklahoma. Somehow, each time we were able to get it fixed, relying on either our own wits or the generosity of strangers. The whole trip was becoming a struggle just to keep the bus moving forward. The goal was to make it to Vermont for a music festival a couple of weeks out.

There was a loud bang, the bus shuddered, and the engine stopped. With flashers blinking we rolled over to the side of the highway.

"Shit! Fuck! Shit!" Cornelius swore repeatedly while gripping the wheel.

When it was clear that the bus wasn't going anywhere, I asked, "What now?"

"I'll have to check under the hood." He wiped the sweat from his forehead, stood up and walked down the two steps.

We followed Cornelius onto the hot pavement in front of the school bus. I had seen the inside of that Ford flathead V8 engine more times than I cared to. Cornelius lifted the hood and hooked the metal rod to keep it open. Reaching his hand, he gave the radiator a slight turn. Steam hissed back at him.

Holding my hair back, I leaned in to get a closer look. Oil was splattered everywhere, but that was normal.

Eight spark plugs hung like spider legs from both sides of the engines head. Cars passed by us in a blur.

Coming back up for air, I asked, "What are we going to do?"

Right on cue, a tow truck pulled up. The driver exited, belly bulging over his belt, a baseball cap pulled down over his eyes. "What seems to be the problem?" He spoke directly to Cornelius.

"She's overheated."

He nodded. "I can tow you to a mechanic nearby for sixty bucks."

Cornelius shuffled back and forth and pushed the center of his glasses up his nose. Diane and I had spent most of our savings on food, though probably a larger chunk had gone to alcohol.

"OK. OK. Let's tow her then." Cornelius shrugged.

"Once I get it hooked up, you two girls get in the bus, and you can get up front with me." He nodded at Cornelius.

There we were, three weary, dusty travelers standing on the side of a busy highway. I was disappointed in the bus for breaking down all the time. It was beginning to feel like I was seeing the inner workings of gas stations instead of the beautiful countryside I had planned for. Hanging my arms limply at my side, the tow-truck driver grabbed a thick hook that hung from a crane off his truck. Lowering himself underneath the bumper, I could see the rolls of flesh of his gross belly as he attached the hook to the axel of the bus. He told us to climb on board and within minutes the front end of the bus was off the ground.

Ten minutes later we rolled into a Shell gas station. There was a canopy over two gas pumps, an office, and lifts for cars in need of repair inside the garage. The driver pulled the bus alongside the bathrooms. Once the truck came to a stop, we joined Cornelius up front.

"Tony will take good care of you," the driver reassured us from under his baseball cap, gesturing to the office.

The office was a small room with papers strewn all over a clunky desk. An adding machine, a rotary phone, a pack of Camels and an ashtray sat on top of the disarray.

"Ello," Tony stood up. He was a middle-aged man in his fifties, round, tan, with a bit of peppered growth across his cheeks. "How a can I help you?"

"Our bus broke down."

"Can't look at it today," Tony said, his Italian accent coming through. "Too busy, but tomorrow I can check it out."

Cornelius explained to him that we were on our way to the east coast.

"You live-a-like-a hippies?" Tony said.

"Yeah, sort of like hippies." Cornelius smiled.

"I bet it's nice a living like that." Tony gazed over Cornelius's shoulder with a smile.

His look was one of yearning, so not to encourage him, I looked away.

"Well-a you can sleep on your bus and use the bathroom here." Tony waved a hand.

We were already indebted to him.

*

The next day we went off on foot to explore Chicago. The gas station was several blocks away from Lake Michigan. We walked past a locksmith, butchers and subway stands. The scent of urine seeped out of certain alleyways. Ultimately, we made it to Lake Shore Drive, where tourists and locals hung around. While many people walked their dogs or jogged, there were also drug dealers selling their wares.

"Ludes. Got ludes here," a guy with a jacket and a shag haircut chanted, his eyes scanning back and forth.

I didn't know then, but Quaaludes were discovered in India in the 1950's, when scientists were looking for a way to fight malaria. By the sixties the unpatented drug had landed in the US to treat insomnia and anxiety. The chalky, white pill with '714' stamped on it, had people taking them at dance clubs and parties, or just to relax. The name Quaaludes came from two words. Quiet and interlude. I wanted whatever that guy had.

"Should we get some?" I whispered.

"No way!" Diane snapped.

"OK. OK." She was still upset about the time I'd passed out and snored all the way through a Joe Cocker concert. It would be a long time before she let that one go.

We returned to the station when the sun was going down. The light had subdued, the sky going to pinks and fading blues.

Tony greeted and let us know he had good news and bad news.

"Give me the good news first," Cornelius said.

"You'll only need a water pump." Tony shrugged.

Cornelius exhaled with relief. "And the bad news?"

"It's gonna take about-a ten days for it to arrive." Tony held his palms up to the sky.

"Now what?" I asked.

"I don't mind you kids staying in your bus while you wait for the part." Tony spoke to Cornelius but smiled directly at me.

"That would be far out, man!" Cornelius said.

"I can even take you all to dinner after I go a home to take a shower," he said.

Of course, being low on cash, we all agreed.

*

When Tony came back, he was dressed in a white Izod polo shirt and a Members Only jacket. His face was freshly shaved and his black hair slicked back.

"Sorry, we don't have any nice clothes with us." I felt underdressed in my jeans and zip-up sweatshirt.

"No clothes?" he said, taking note.

A cab took us past graffiti lined store fronts where hookers stalked the streets in tiny outfits and high boots. A few minutes later we arrived at a non-descript store front.

"This is my favorite place to getta real Italian meal." Like a Hollywood version of Italian appreciation, Tony pinched all his fingers together and kissed them to the air.

The round tables were covered in traditional red and white checkered table clothes. The maître-d, dressed in a black suit, white shirt and bowtie welcomed us.

"Ah Tony, Tony, Tony! So good to see you, my friend." Air kisses to both cheeks. "You have brought new friends, I see?"

"Yes, these guys are hippies all the way from-a California."

"Well, any friend of Tony's is a friend of mine," he said, shaking each of our hands, a smile on his face. He led us to a table in the corner, plucking the Reserved placard as he motioned us to the chairs.

"Your favorite table for my favorite customer sir."

"Grazie, grazie," Tony said.

Tony acted like a mafia don who knew everyone. Waiters and patrons alike stopped to say hello as they walked by.

The waiter took our order, or more accurately, Tony ordered spaghetti and ravioli for everyone. A strikingly handsome busboy delivered a bottle of wine, a basket of fresh baked Italian bread, and olive oil to our table. Tall, dark and handsome--just the way I liked them. I secretly wished I could see what his story was, but I knew better than to flirt in front of our gracious host. Though nothing between us had been established, I intuited that my attention shouldn't be delivered anywhere else. Glasses of wine were poured and we all toasted with Tony, "To new friends." Once again, I made up an excuse and told myself it was okay to drink because I couldn't insult our gracious host, and we were in Chicago, after all.

"So, Tony why did you come to America?" Diane asked.

"Well, I love America very much," he said. "Many of my family was already here. My brother, Vinnie came first sponsored by my cousin. I work-a...with cars in Italy so I told my brother, I want a gas a station in the USA. Since my cousin brought him, it was now his responsibility to help me start my own business here."

On my second glass of wine the entree came. We all started spinning our forks in long strands of spaghetti, heavily sauced and boldly spiced. Unashamed, Tony sucked a single strand between his lips.

"So, your brother bought you the gas station?" Diane asked.

"He loaned me the money, and now I must bring someone else over from the old country and help them get started."

"Far fucking out, dude," Cornelius said, his general response to most situations.

Tony laughed. "It is a... far fucking out."

"If only everyone helped each other like that," I said.

"We Italians do favors for one another," Tony winked.

"Like the Godfather," Diane said.

Tony's brow furrowed, but he didn't respond. I paused, hoping she hadn't crossed some invisible line. But as the wine started to hit me, I was getting looser by the minute. I could tell Diane was feeling it, too.

"What about you girls? What do you do in California?"

"We work in a 24-hour restaurant, but we saved our money so we could travel this summer."

"Ah, I want to see America. I like how you do it. In a bus." Tony smiled at Cornelius.

"The bus is cool, man," Cornelius said.

"Very cool, man," Tony said.

Later that evening, Tony had the taxi drop us off back at the station. We didn't question his hospitality, as he gave each of us air kisses on both cheeks. When it was my turn, he pulled me in with my hand and held it a little longer than the others, tracing his thumb across my palm. While I wanted to tell him to stop, no one had taught me how.

*

The days waiting for the bus part to arrive ticked by. Sometimes we'd hang out near the lake, sometimes we'd drink too much and pass out. Sitting still reminded me of my time in juvenile hall. I wanted to hit the road.

It was on one of those boring days that I gazed out the window of the bus and saw Tony talking to two cops in front of their patrol car. My first thought was maybe he was making some kind of report. But then he reached deep into his front pocket, pulled a wad of cash out and handed it to one of them. My heart took off. Maybe I was seeing something that I wasn't supposed to see. Instinctively, I lowered down in my seat. After the police left, I woke Diane up from her nap and described the scene. "Tony is in the mob," I said.

"Did he see you watching him?" Diane asked.

"No. No. I was hiding."

"We better not piss him off."

For days, Tony had been making advances toward me. He winked so much, I thought maybe he had some sort of tic. He was always tilting his head sideways to get a better look at my ass whenever I walked by. At first, I tried ignoring his flirtations. But a few days later, I was coming out of the restroom, and Tony was there.

"Oh, hi, Tony."

"You-a... need some new clothes, I think," he said, looking me up and down. It was true. I had lost over twenty pounds from the dysentery I caught in Wyoming, and as result my clothes barely fit anymore.

"I don't have enough money for that."

"I buy you an outfit so you can look nice when I take you out again."

Biting the inside of my lower lip, I pulled on a stand of my long brown hair. All of a sudden, Tony reached his hand around my lower back, and pressed me to him. He put his mouth over mine. The kiss happened too quick to process.

"Uh, Tony, your customers," I said, pulling back.

"I no care about customers. I like you." Tony pulled out a hundred-dollar bill. "Go buy you-a little something nice to wear."

"Oh, you don't have to do that..."

"I insist."

I looked at the hundred-dollar bill that had somehow made its way into my hand. Some threshold was being crossed. I felt it. "Thanks, Tony."

I bought a cute, printed flannel pullover top and shorts that better showed my new figure. The next day I wanted to show Tony the purchase, so he'd know the money had gone to good use. When I approached Tony, he quickly led me to a dingy room in the back where a small bunk was crammed up against the wall. I knew it was my turn to pay the favor back.

He set me down on the edge of the bunk and pulled off my shorts and panties.

"Ah, Tony, I don't know if..."

"You are just the way I like my women. Nice and thick."

I gazed at the exit. Should I make a run for it? Should I yell for help? I did none of those things because I still hadn't learned to say no to a man, and instead I remarked, "What if someone comes in?"

"Don't worry, I locked the door." In an instant, he was in me and humping away. His stale, old breath on my face. I didn't want to look at the middle-aged man on top of me, so I closed my eyes. I didn't think about getting pregnant either. Thank God it was over quickly. A few moments later, we were smoking with Tony's round belly resting against my ribs. The smell of motor oil fumes hung in the air, and the taste of shame rose up in the back of my throat.

"I want to get you an apartment," he said. "I will take care of you and pay all your bills."

I already knew what the conditions would be. I would have to have sex with him whenever he wanted, and in return I would be a kept woman. While I was disgusted by the idea, I was also tempted by it as well. I was just beginning to learn, even if I had no self-worth to speak of, my body had its own monetary value. There was a part of me that longed to start a new life somewhere where no one knew me and I didn't have a rap sheet anymore. It would also be nice to not have to work again. "But...but what about my sister?"

"She can stay, too." He smiled.

I felt like I was being offered my own leading role in the Godfather. All of Gretchen's acting lessons were finally pay off.

Later, when I told Diane about Tony's offer, she went off. "Are you crazy? No way!"

"But he said, he'd pay for both of us."

"You'd have to sleep with him all the time."

Hearing her say it out loud, made me feel disgusting. I was a tramp. I lowered my head.

Thankfully, the water pump arrived two days later and we got the bus fixed. Later, when it was time to say good-bye, Tony gripped my hand in his. "I no charge you, but I want you to stay with me."

My eyes came up to meet his. His rough face gleamed with expectation.

"I can't, but I'll call you after our trip, and maybe I can come back then."

"You promise?"

Wearing the new flannel shirt he had bought me, I said, "Yes. I promise."

But of course, I never called.

Night Life

The three of us would drink anywhere, but sometimes we craved the atmosphere of a dive bar with beer-soaked sawdust on the floor. This was the case when Cornelius, Diane and I were passing through Springfield Massachusetts, a state where the drinking age was 18.

The challenge was finding the right bar with the right music and the right people, but you never knew until you stepped inside. They were itching for a little rock, but I preferred Motown to dance to. Driving down a side street, a bright red neon sign beamed Woody's Bar above a non-descript store front. Several people decked out in their Friday-night attire slipped in the front door.

"This looks like it could be good," Cornelius said, pulling over to the side of the road.

In single file, the three of us entered the dimly lit bar and my eyes slowly became accustomed to the flashing strobe lights. Writhing bodies packed on a small dance floor, sweat and sex hung in the air. This wasn't the type of place you'd ever be foolish enough to show up in flip-flops. But after being on the road for over two months I stopped caring as much. Barry White's, "What am I Going to do With You" voice vibrated from every speaker.

"Far fucking out," Cornelius said.

"Let's get a drink," Diane yelled, hands cupped around mouth.

At the bar I ordered a White Russian from a hairy-chested guy with a gold chain dangling around his neck. When he handed me a glass, I noticed his dark hairy knuckles. I gulped down half my drink. "I have to go to the bathroom," I yelled over the music.

Diane followed me behind a red velvet curtain down a dark corridor to the end of the hall. I pushed the restroom door and popped into one of the stalls. She did the same. I studied the graffiti while I released a steady stream into the bowl. Names and numbers were scribbled on the wall. "Looking for a good time, call Joe at..." or "SUCK MY COCK" and other tacky invitations for cheap fun.

When I stepped out of the stall there was a woman at the mirror in a tight pink dress and a cheap wig smudging eyeliner across her lids, a cigarette dangling from her lips. Diane came out just after me.

"Hey girl." Hot Pink's voice was a gravely male voice. It was a man in full drag.

"Ah... hi?" I said.

Hot Pink turned around and smiled. "Just think of me as one of the girls."

I giggled nervously, never having encountered an actual drag queen before. "Oh. Okay." I said, before she clicked out in her high heels.

Diane covered her mouth with a hand, eyes opened wide.

"I think this is a gay bar," I whispered.

How had we not noticed it was a gay bar? I wasn't looking for it. My eyes or mind or both had adjusted to my narrow band width of experience. At the time, gay bars in many states were illegal and were often targets of violence.

The door opened and another two queens came in. One in tight jeans and black eye liner, the other in a tight blue sweater.

"Girl, did you see Mikey walk in?" Tight jeans asked. "He's so damn hot."

Diane and I rushed down the corridor and back to Cornelius.

"We're in a gay bar," I said.

"Yeah, I know." Cornelius shrugged.

"Why didn't you tell us?"

"I just figured it out when someone pinched my ass."

We both cracked up. It was refreshing to see Cornelius being targeted for a change.

The three of us stood there sipping our drinks as people moved on the small squared-off dance floor. The smell of beer and smoke hovered below the ceiling like its own weather system. We were in a vortex. My hips began to sway with the music. When the speakers thumped with the sound of the Staple Singers, I could no longer contain myself.

"Let's dance." I pulled Diane by the wrist.

Seconds later we were crammed between dozens of sweaty strangers. Everyone was having so much fun. It was contagious. Diane and I started bouncing the sides of our hips together, doing The Bump.

Someone shoved Amyl Nitrate under my nose. I didn't ask what it was, I just knew to inhale. In an instant a warm rush flooded my senses. My lips went numb. My mouth wet. When I looked around everyone was pressing poppers into each other's faces. My eyes drifted to a guy with hair so gelled it looked like a swim-cap. Someone in cheetah-patterned pants was moving in slow motion. Men were kissing each other on the mouth. Intoxicated by it all, it seemed like the most natural thing on earth. Maybe it was the alcohol or maybe the poppers, but I felt safe on that dance floor. These men wanted nothing from me. Wanted nothing from Diane. Their eyes weren't hungrily roving my body. They weren't making propositions or inappropriately touching me in places I didn't want them to. I didn't have to be on guard.

When Macarena started playing everyone fell into formation in rows across the dance floor. Diane and I had so much fun learning the steps. And years later when gay bars finally became legal, they would be the place I would often go.

Crossing All Boundaries

It had been eleven weeks on the road, and Diane and I were tired of sleeping on mattresses that smelled of piss and beer. Tired of showering in college locker rooms, random campsites or sometimes not showering at all. Tired of driving hundreds of miles for a music festival that disappointed with local garage bands. We were just about to call it quits when Cornelius came up with another idea. "We should head on down to New Orleans."

Cornelius had regaled us with tales of round-the-clock nightlife, live jazz and the vibrant music scene in the Big Easy. While part of us wanted to go home, the vagabond life can get in your bloodstream. At the time, it sounded like the perfect destination for two young girls wanting to see the world.

"Let's do it," Diane said, and I quickly agreed.

From Vermont we headed south on Route 5. Diane and I sat up front, feet propped up on the safety bar, scanning for any hitchhikers on the side of the road. Getting gas money from riders was just one way we kept the bus moving. We had done other things that I wouldn't normally do. In St. Louis we sold plasma for twenty-five bucks. I damn near passed out after they pulled those three cups from my body. Another time we were so desperate we called Dad begging for money.

He reluctantly wired us a hundred bucks but told us not to ask again.

I looked down at my firm legs sprouting out of my cut-off jeans, pleased that they weren't as plump as they had been when we left home. I could thank the dysentery for finally getting me to my ideal body weight. As a result, I no longer had to drape myself in oversized t-shirts. I was no longer eating candy and Cheetos all day. And while my compulsion for food had gone away, my drinking consumption was worse than ever. I was starting to see a pattern. When I drank I often lost control. Usually, I just wanted to get a buzz, but I always seemed to miss my mark. If there was a bottle of wine and no one else was drinking it (which was rare), I would finish it. After all, I couldn't let it go to waste. I usually ended up in a partial black out, making thick-tongued exclamations of how much 'I love you' to anyone that happened to be around. The next day I would be embarrassed when someone would tell me of my obnoxious behavior. The feelings I had of self-loathing often caused me to get something else to drink to make them go away. It was a vicious cycle. One that I didn't understand, nor could I stop.

I told myself one day it would be different. One day I would go back to school. One day, I would meet someone, fall in love and I wouldn't feel so all alone anymore. That's when I would really start living my life.

Just outside of Hartford, Connecticut, I was brought back to the present when the bus lurched and snapped my neck forward. There was a loud bang and the engine died.

"Fuck! Fuck! Fuck!" Cornelius span the wheel with both hands, maneuvering the bus to the side of the road. When he got us out of harm's way, his chin fell to his chest.

"Now what?" I snapped.

Cornelius pushed himself up and made his way down the two steps. Diane and I followed behind. Cars and trucks were zipping by in a blur on the highway next to us. We gazed under the hood. None of us knew what we were looking for, but that's just what you do when you break down on the road.

An hour later we were being towed to a local gas station where we met the owner, Tom, who was dressed in grease-spotted overalls. "What seems to be the problem folks?" He wiped his oily hands on his pant legs.

"We'd appreciate it if you could take a look at our bus and tell us, Tom," Cornelius said.

"Sure thing, but you might want to get yourself a coffee while you wait."

We strolled down the block to a diner. We sat in a vinyl booth studying the laminated menu. With great consideration of our limited funds, we decided on a special they offered of chicken fried steak with soup and salad.

"Maybe it will be something minor this time," Cornelius said, reaching across the table for the salt.

"But how are we going to pay for it?" Diane asked.

"We should just go home Diane," I said.

Diane gave me a little eye roll, indicating she didn't want to talk about that in front of Cornelius at that particular moment.

When we got back to the station Tom said, "Well, guys it seems your bus has blown a gasket."

I had no idea what a gasket was, but I could tell by Cornelius's defeated look it was not good. "If you want me to fix it, the part will take a few days to get here."

"How much, Tom?" Cornelius asked.

"One hundred and fifty dollars, that includes parts and labor."

"Well, we don't have any choice," Cornelius said.

"Can we sleep on the bus Tom?" I asked.

Tom gave each of us the once over. "Sure. Not a problem." He shrugged.

Being broke down in random towns brought on bone-crushing boredom. I mean, how much can one entertain themselves on a bus? On the second day, we were sitting around filling up on mini-donuts and Coca-Cola when there was a tap on the door. It was Ben, a local man around forty, with dark almond skin, who owned a U-Haul business close by. Tom had told him about our dire circumstances.

"I heard you guys broke down?" Ben asked.

"Yeah. We break down all the time." I shrugged.

"I hear y'all are traveling to New Orleans?"

"That was the plan," Diane said.

"I was there once and I loved it." He gazed into the distance, bringing up some memory that we weren't privy to.

After that, Ben started to come by every day after he got off work. He brought us soda, fruit and on a couple of glorious occasions, pizza. He always seemed interested and inquired about all our adventures, like he was living vicariously through us. He said he wished he could travel but that he had too many responsibilities in his life now.

At first, we thought Ben just wanted to help us out, until the fourth day, when Diane and I were alone with him.

"I think I know how I could help you girls out." Ben stood up front in khaki pants with his index finger to his chin.

"Oh really. How?" I asked.

"How about you two girls sleep with me?" He looked back and forth to Diane and then at me. "I'll pay you each seventy-five bucks."

"Oh my god. That is so gross!" Diane said.

"We are sisters Ben," I said.

"I've always had a fantasy about being with two sisters."

"No fucking way!" I exclaimed.

"Okay. Okay." He raised his hands in surrender. "Just trying to help you girls."

The proposal hung in the air, like stink from a steaming pile of shit, until he apologized and took off for the night.

When Cornelius came back, we told him what happened. He sat on a mattress, looking like he was mulling it over. "If it was me, I would do it."

I looked over at Diane who rolled her eyes in disgust.

"It's easy money." He shrugged.

"That's because you're a guy," I said. By that time my resentments were building with Cornelius. I had busted him in Chicago trying to take advantage of Diane when she was passed out drunk. I told him to knock that crap off, which he quickly did. But it was too late, I had learned then Cornelius was an opportunist who would take advantage of us given half the chance.

The next day, Cornelius had conveniently disappeared again when Ben came back. "Brought you guys something to eat," he said, climbing on board.

I wondered what the pervert wanted now? Sure enough, after a few minutes, he was propositioning us again. "I feel really bad for you girls. I really want to help you all, so I was thinking, what if I paid each of you a hundred bucks? That would give you some money to enjoy your trip."

"We're not doing that, so forget it," Diane said firmly.

Again, Ben raised his hands in mock-surrender. But as another two days of excruciating boredom ticked by the subject got picked up by me and Diane.

"I wonder what it would be like to actually do it with Ben?" Diane asked.

"Gross, but the money would help us out."

"But he's so old." Diane scrunched up her face in disgust. "He's got to be over forty."

"You could keep your eyes closed during it." I laughed.

"The money would cover the cost of getting the bus fixed," Diane said.

The following day Ben came by again. Cornelius conveniently had something to do and left us alone.

"Howdy girls." He sat down on the front seat. "I've been thinking. What if I gave you each one hundred and fifty bucks?"

This time there was silence.

"You'll not only have enough money to pay for repairs, but you'll have pocket money for the rest of your trip."

Diane and I gazed at each other.

"Hypothetically, if we did say yes, where would we do it at?" I asked.

He moved in a little closer, eyes glistening with expectation. "I could get us a room at a motel not far from here."

I took a drag of my cigarette, imaging myself naked with this man. But I had already done it with Tony, so how bad could it actually be? Maybe we were just being a couple of prudish former Catholic girls, and maybe Cornelius was right when he said, it was just sex.

"I'll pay you both in cash"

Diane and I locked eyes with one another and gave each other a nod.

"Okay, then. Come back tomorrow," I said.

Clapping his hands, he rubbed them briskly together. "See you tomorrow after work then"

The next day, Diane and I both sat in Ben's pickup truck. Diane kept elbowing me in my ribs, but it was too late. Ben drove to a motel off the main road a mile away and parked the truck, disappearing into the office.

"Are you sure you want to do this?" Diane asked.

"No. I don't want to do it, but we need the money."

When the driver's door opened again, Ben dangled a red diamond shaped keyring in between his fingers. "We're all set girls."

We followed Ben into the dimly-lit room with thick maroon curtains. When I saw the massive king-sized bed, I told myself it wasn't too late to change my mind. But I wanted the money more than I wanted to maintain any thread of self-respect. Which was already frayed pretty thin.

I took a shower and wrapped myself in a towel. Diane was sitting in a chair, already draped in a towel. Beaming, Ben was in the middle of the bed, patting both sides of the mattress. "Come on in girls. The water is fine."

Diane and I looked at each other before dropping the towels and climbing in on either side of him.

Ben's eyes burned with heat as his head went back and forth.

"Now what?" I asked.

"Somebody get me hard."

"I'll do it." Diane took a deep dive under the covers with the volunteerism of a patriot doing what was necessary for their country. My head was racing. What the fuck were we doing? This was so fucking gross.

Ben moaned, pulling me to his side. His dark skin smelled of baby powder. I could see Diane's head bobbing up and down under the blanket below. After a few minutes, Ben said, "Okay, Diane... that's good."

With a quick flip Ben was on top of me, pushing himself inside without a condom, while Diane watched with deep concern from the other side. I went somewhere far away in my head. Far away from the heat of his body, the dark maroon curtains, the smell of sweat. I disassociated just like I used to do when Mom would have one of her breakdowns. My mind imagining what New Orleans would be like once we got there. The music, the people and the fun we would have with kids our own age.

Thank God, it was over fast. Ben was moaning and on his back between us. "Did you come?" Diane asked.

"Oh yeah, baby. I came alright."

I grabbed a cigarette, facing the window, and took a deep inhale.

"I hope you girls enjoyed that as much as I did?"

"Yeah. It was great," I mumbled, taking another hit. The insistence that men want to know if women enjoyed a sexual act, even if they had paid for it, was a mystery to me.

"Let me go clean up." I watched as Ben's muscular ass headed for the bathroom.

"It wasn't that bad, was it?" Diane said.

"It was pretty gross." I shook my head, feeling like I had lost another piece of myself in that sweaty bed.

"We can never, ever tell anyone this happened," Diane said.

"Are you kidding? Never!"

Diane and I were dressed when Ben came out of the bathroom wrapped in a towel. All I wanted to do was to get the money and get the hell out of that hotel. Ben had a black vinyl money pouch in his hand. He momentarily paused before unzipping it and started to dig inside. When his hand came back out, he was holding a bronze badge cupped in the palm of his hand. "Girls, I'm with the FBI and you both are under arrest."

Diane jumped up, "What? Why are you doing...Oh my God!"

"What the fuck?" My heart leaped clear to my throat. I looked toward the door, but I knew there was no way we could get out of there now. Neither of us had any time to engage our logic. No time to reason that the FBI isn't going to be interested in two young girls on the road. I thought we were headed to jail for prostitution, even though none of it made any sense.

Diane started to cry, and I was on the verge when Ben laughed. "I'm just playing with you girls. I'm not with the FBI."

I grabbed my chest and tightened my lips. "You fucker! That was so mean."

"That was not funny at all, Ben." Diane yelled.

"Okay, okay. I'm sorry." Ben must have realized his mistake and quickly pulled out three crisp hundred-dollar bills and laid them neatly on the bed. "Let me make it up to you girls."

"I can't believe you would do that," I said, retrieving the cash.

Angry, Diane and I washed up in the bathroom. And a few minutes later we were driving back to the bus, enduring an awkward silence. When Ben dropped us off, it was the last time we saw him. Apparently, he didn't need to come back. He had already gotten what he came for. We didn't tell Cornelius the details, but he knew. How else would we magically come up with the money to pay for the repairs of the bus? In fact, it would be decades before Diane and I would ever talk about it again.

But the road trip and all its initial innocence was over, even if I didn't know it yet.

Homeward Bound

The trip came to a screeching halt when the bus's engine blew up in Maryland, just past the Mason Dixon Line. Cornelius, Diane and I watched as the tow truck lifted the school bus to take it to its final resting place. I felt a strange, unexpected sadness, as it disappeared down the road. I imagined it going to a junkyard where other battered vehicles were being picked over for parts. I imagined it becoming rusty with old age, weeds growing up around its flat tires. Gone were the days of laughter and music that echoed from those metal walls. Gone were the festivals, the hippies and the outcasts chasing far-fetched dreams of adventure. No one would ever know how much fun it provided, the miles it had traveled, or the desperate acts two particular girls would do to get it rolling again.

"That's it then?" Cornelius looked from Diane to me, and back to Diane. At that point I was well aware that he was a manipulator and not falling for anymore cons.

"We're going home," I said.

"Maybe we could stay at my friend's house down in New Orleans...."

By then I was done with his charms, manipulations and vagabond ways. Instead, Diane and I stuck out our thumbs, and seeing it was pointless to argue further, Cornelius joined us.

We asked our first ride to drop us off at a truck stop on I-80 in order to find someone traveling across the country. The truck stop was a beehive of activity with semi-trucks pulling in and out, air brakes hissing, and travelers stopping in for something to eat at the diner. While trying to decide our next move, we couldn't help but notice a bus that had "Grey Rabbit" stenciled in black on its side.

The Grey Rabbit bus line was an underground company founded in 1971. It provided trips from San Francisco to New York on a weekly basis for fifty-five bucks. The seats on the bus were removed and replaced with wall-to-wall mattresses. At one point the company was making $40,000 a summer, until complaints about buses being too crowded or breaking down with no backup plan started to circulate.

Not hesitating, Cornelius walked right up to the hippie driver fueling his tank. "Hey man, do you think we can get a ride?"

Squinting the driver looked us up and down. "Can you chip in anything for gas?"

"Man, I totally would if I could, but we're completely broke."

He pulled the gas nozzle from the tank and put it back. "I've got paying passengers on board, so I'd really have to ask them."

"Really appreciate it if you would, man," Cornelius said.

The three of us followed the driver onto the bus where around twenty passengers were scattered on mattresses or the front seats.

"These folks need a ride, but they don't have any money. Are you guys okay with them hitching a ride with us?" Cornelius looked over the driver's shoulder with a forlorn expression on his face. I recognized that look because I had seen it many times when he was trying to get his way.

All the riders chimed in saying "yes" "sure" "of course" "welcome on board."

"Far fucking out man," Cornelius said, taking an empty seat in front. Diane and I went to the back and plopped down on one of the mattresses.

It was three quick days, sometimes driving through the night. We arrived in San Francisco where we were dropped off downtown. As we secured the straps of our packs around our waists, Cornelius surprised us. "I'm going to stay here with some friends for a while," he said.

"You're not coming to L.A. with us?" Diane asked.

"It turns out I might have a gig at a local joint."

Cornelius often talked about the days he played backup guitar for mainstream rock bands, but it was hard to imagine because I only knew him as a bus driver.

"We're going to miss you." Diane teared up.

"I will call you when I get back into town." He gave us each a hug.

"Thanks for everything Cornelius," she said.

"Yeah. Thanks for everything."

By the end of our travels I had built up enough resentments against Cornelius that I didn't miss seeing him go. At the time, I thought he had been using us to lure guys in to pay for gas, to buy food, or even pay us to have sex with them. I realize now that if the bus hadn't picked us up in New Mexico, there would have been no Rainbow Festival, no Central City and no taking in the gorgeous landscape of the country. We found a sense of security with Cornelius and his bus because it provided a home base.

After Cornelius walked away, Diane and I stuck out our thumbs. Later, we would hear that he was still traveling and playing music gigs from our mutual friends, but we would never actually see him again.

We quickly got a ride from some old dude heading south on the 101. Diane sat up front while I crawled in the back. There were several hours of mindless chitchat. When I gazed out the window at one point, I noticed a sign that said, Atascadero State Hospital. My mind traveled back to when I was a teenager at Camarillo hospital and Dad took me out on a pass. Instead of going somewhere fun we ended up going to visit my brother, Jay, who was an inmate at the maximum-security facility for the criminally insane. He landed up there following a series of bad choices stemming back to when he was manufacturing LSD in our house. While the charges were dropped at that time, he got picked up a second time. During his incarceration, a psychiatrist diagnosed him as a paranoid schizophrenic. And from there he was sentenced to Atascadero for three years.

It didn't occur to me that my poor dad was dealing with two kids in mental institutions at the same time. Hadn't he already been through enough with a wife who had killed herself and left him to raise four children alone?

Apparently not.

When we got to Santa Monica our ride dropped us off at Diane's house and she drove me home in her Bahama yellow Volkswagen. As we pulled up to the little house on Stanford, I had mixed feelings. While I was longing for a cozy bed and a hot shower, just being around my dad could bristle me to the core.

"You really need to get out of here." Diane said, before I got out.

While that was something I was longing for, I didn't know how to pull it off. "Like where am I supposed to live?"

"We could get a place together."

In many ways Diane and I had become like escape artists trying to flee the suffocation of our childhoods. Perhaps we thought if we traveled far enough and drank hard enough maybe the pain of losing our mother at an early age would go away. After the bonding of the road trip Diane wanted to help me escape. For now, I had to stay with Dad.

"I'll call you," I said, giving her a hug.

Dad was sitting at the small dining room table. The television was blasting the news. When he saw me, he got up and gave me a hug. "Welcome home," he said.

His hair was salt and pepper. His brown eyes had become hooded, his skin brown and weathered from time. He wasn't even sixty yet, but he looked extremely old. "How was your trip?"

"It was cool. We got to see a lot of the country."

"Want to join me for some spaghetti dinner?"

"Sure, after I clean up." He was being super nice.

Standing under the shower I washed away the dirt and grime from the trip. I scrubbed so hard my flesh turned a bright red. I wanted to remove the traces of the men I had slept with. The bad decisions I had made. I wanted to wash away my fucked-up life. I wanted to disappear.

Later, when I came back into the living room Dad, not having any idea how much I hated being there, had a big smile on his face. "You'll never guess what," he said.

"What, Dad?" I sighed.

"I stopped drinking while you were gone." He held a glass of orange juice up as proof.

How had he been able to quit when I couldn't get through a city or state without a drink? Had we simply gotten to the point of switching roles? Was I turning into fragmented pieces of both my mother and my father?

"But how? Why?" I asked.

"I have cirrhosis of the liver."

I wasn't quite sure what cirrhosis was, but apparently at fifty-five Dad's liver was badly scarred. "So, you just stopped?"

"I didn't have a choice."

I couldn't wrap my head around his "not having a choice." I felt the opposite. I had to get high. My very life depended on it. If I wasn't turning off the critical, self-defeating voices in my head, I would have surely killed myself a long time ago. Drugs and alcohol were the very thing that was keeping me alive.

As we sat at the dining room table spinning long strands of spaghetti on forks it was hard to find anything meaningful to say. Even if I wanted to be closer to my father, at that point neither of us could navigate the empty space that laid between us. There were no road maps with county lines to cross, no coast to reach and no redeeming festivals to attend. It was the same old story–concealment, with invisible rigid boundaries, booby trapped with secrets and lies. And while Dad had always had his secrets, now, I had my own.

Epilogue

It's a Monday night and I'm sitting in my living room, logging into a virtual support group that I facilitate every week. I wave at the dozen teens on my screen who are sitting in a circle at a residential treatment center across town. As they wave back, I can't tell if they're smiling because they're all wearing masks.

"Hi guys, can y'all check in with your names and what brought you here?" I say, to get things rolling.

As they go around the circle one girl with pink hair says, "I'm here for anxiety," another shares, "I'm here for a suicide attempt." They continue: "Trauma;" "Self-harm;" "Depression;" "Substance abuse;" "Eating disorder;" and the list goes on as they all check in.

No one can deny that 2020 was brutal. Kobe Bryant and his daughter dying in a helicopter crash was the first of it. Shortly after that we were all sent to our rooms when Covid19 hit. In lock down, we watched in horror as a police officer killed George Floyd, and riots spread across the country as quickly as the fires raging in the west. The events we witnessed on the evening news were horrific, but one thing we didn't see were all the teens who were suffering behind closed doors.

It's a miracle I survived my adolescence. It's a wonder I survived at all. Shortly after the road trip, I got back together with Max. We ended up strung out on heroin, getting married, having kids until later it imploded and we got a divorce.

On that night of the party, back when I did LSD, our friend Adam snapped photos of all of us with his cherished Minolta 16 EE camera. When I look at the picture now everyone's eyes are red in the photos from the flash of his camera, like some kind of eerie omen that we couldn't see.

Holding that camera as the self-designated memory keeper, Adam had no idea that he would die from an overdose of heroin in his mid-twenties. When it happened, all of us were shocked. We showed up at his funeral just like we had to his party, saying things like, "But he was so young," and "He had so much to live for." And as tragic as it all was, the impact of Adam's early death wouldn't slow me and Max down. It wouldn't make a dent.

Diane went to school to become an R.N. and after a while it became too painful for her to watch her little sister killing herself with drugs, so eventually she stopped all communication with me for several years. In 1980, my Dad died from a bad heart and other complications. I missed the opportunity to say goodbye. I missed out on a lot of things in my unrelenting loop of addiction and incarceration. Writing this book during the pandemic I was surprised to discover a direct portal to my father. The more I examined my youth, the more I realized how he must have lived in a constant state of anxiety and dread with a daughter completely out of control. But what I didn't expect: as I explored my past through writing, I began to see what a jerk I had been.

And it was in that deep self-reflection that I was able to access compassion for my Dad.

In the early nineties, after going to jail for the last time, I decided to get sober. At the beginning I couldn't understand why I had gone through everything I had. Then one day I was asked to speak at Sylmar Juvenile Hall. As I stood there telling my story to incarcerated girls in the same dayroom where I had learned to do the Cha-Cha decades before, I knew I had gone through everything for a purpose, if I was willing to use my life-experience to help someone else.

In the Zoom group after everyone has checked in, I tell them what it was like for me as a teenager. "I felt alone. I had no one to talk to. I turned to drugs to numb the pain." Their heads bob up and down as they relate. As I share my past, it's almost as if time collapses, and I'm reaching back to recover the parts of me I lost along the way. I am reclaiming the younger version of myself. The girl I abandoned every time I took a drink. The one I deserted whenever I was doing drugs. The one who couldn't say 'no' and would give herself away.

If only I knew back then that there were others in the world who were hurting like me, perhaps I wouldn't have done all those crazy things. But the beautiful thing about life is that people can change. The catalyst for that change may come as a result of some leveling circumstances like going to a treatment center, a juvenile hall or a jail. It might come from the despair you feel deep in your gut. My motivation came from the simple desire to be a better mother to my own two boys and to change the trajectory of my family's lineage from mental illness and addiction to one of recovery and healing.

I'm grateful that I learned that life is more like a moving picture show, rather than one still photograph frozen in time.

I hope we all get the opportunity to tip the cosmic scales toward ultimate redemption.

I hope we can all find it in our hearts to forgive.

I hope we all get a chance to heal.

I wrote this book for the kids in my group. I wrote it for the ones in juvenile hall. I wrote it for the ones I'll never meet and for the girl who reads it and realizes she's not alone.

She's just like me.

Acknowledgements

First off, I would not have written this book without the Big Pause of Covid19, so thank you 2020 lock down for helping me get it done.

I want to acknowledge the three incredible editors who were each stepping stones in my creative process. First, I want to thank Rena Gallagher who helped me bring it to form. Then the amazing, Kelly Hartog who meticulously finetuned the chapters. And finally, Shawna Kenney, a truly gifted editor who helped me bring it to its best possible incarnation. Thank you all for your diligence and care in getting this story told.

Thank you to my brilliant publishers, Rob and Christine Roth for your belief in my writing. And thank you to Gregory & Michelle for your support.

Thank you to my first writing teacher, Karin Gutman whose workshops and impeccable boundaries gave me a safe place to find my voice.

Thank you to all the amazing friends and colleagues who have been there for me throughout the years. As much of a bad ass as I thought I was, I had no defense against your kindness, and for that I am truly grateful to each and every one of you.

Thank you to Kat Ditty and Molly Jordan for your time and feedback on my book.

I also want to thank and acknowledge all of my colleagues at Polaris Teen Center, who have created a space where troubled adolescents can begin the healing process. Your integrity, commitment, and devotion inspires me. And let me thank each one of the warriors out there on the front lines of mental health who give their time and energy in helping individuals get to the other side.

Thank you to my grandchildren, Alyssa, Mariah, Marc and Matthew. I'm deeply proud of you all. And finally – I want to thank my two boys, Jerry and Rikki, I'm so proud of the men you've become.

Love to you all.

About The Author

Wendy Adamson currently works at a treatment center for adolescents struggling with mental health issues, and volunteers her free time to Hav A Sole, a non-profit that delivers quality tennis shoes to the underserved. Committed to breaking the stigma of mental illness and addiction, Wendy has told her stories from prison, the stage and can sometimes be heard on the radio.